A DAY
OF SOLEMN
THANKSGIVING

*Moravian Music
for the Fourth of July, 1783,
in Salem, North Carolina*

A DAY
OF SOLEMN
THANKSGIVING

by MARILYN GOMBOSI

The University of North Carolina Press · Chapel Hill

Music autography by Helen M. Jenner

Copyright © 1977 by
The University of North Carolina Press
All rights reserved

Manufactured in the United States of America
Library of Congress Catalog Card Number 76-6533
ISBN 0-8078-1275-7

Library of Congress Cataloging in Publication Data

Gombosi, Marilyn.
  A day of solemn thanksgiving.

  1. Church music—Moravian Church. 2. Moravians
in North Carolina. I. Title.
ML200.7.N8G6   783'.026'46   76-6533
ISBN 0-8078-1275-7

CONTENTS

ILLUSTRATIONS

$\mathcal{CRC}$PREFACE

For students of American history and culture, there is a gold mine to be found in the archives of the Moravian Church in America. The voluminous records collected and preserved in the Moravian Archives in Winston-Salem, North Carolina, and its northern counterpart in Bethlehem, Pennsylvania, provide continuing eyewitness accounts of every facet of life in the American Moravian communities, illuminating a small but significant part of this country's story from the early years of the eighteenth century to the present. There has been a continuing effort during this century to collect and organize the early records of the Moravians and to make them available for research. Written in German script and preserved in manuscript form, the original documents are being translated and published with regularity. The vast musical holdings of the early Moravians, consisting of thousands of manuscript scores and parts, have been placed in the custody of The Moravian Music Foundation, Incorporated, an organization charged with preserving, collecting, and editing the music and encouraging musicological research in the music archives.

While engaged in these activities as assistant director of the foundation, I became increasingly interested in the restoration projects conducted under the auspices of Old Salem, Incorporated, the agency responsible for supervising the restoration of the eighteenth-century village of Salem, which is now part of Winston-Salem, North Carolina. Working from documents in the Moravian Archives, researchers plan and execute the restoration of a building to its original structure, complete and accurate to the smallest detail, and equip it with either its original furnishings or appropriate pieces of the period. Complementing the building restoration is a program of interpretation, also based on information contained in the Moravian records, that concentrates on the people who once lived and worked in those buildings, explaining their customs and attitudes and illustrating the activities that occupied their lives. Thus the restoration area, which could be merely a collection of quaint buildings, has become a living eighteenth-century village. To spend a day in Old Salem is to relive one day in its history.

While observing the restoration techniques practiced by my colleagues in Old Salem, I began to consider how the same techniques could be applied to research in Moravian music. To the modern catalogs of music manuscripts, the studies of individual composers and their works, and the histories of musical organizations and their libraries, we could add a new area of research focused on recreating specific musical events that occurred in the various Moravian communities during the eighteenth century. This new area of musical research would require its own methodology that could be adapted from the existing procedures followed in building restorations. After selection of the musical event to be restored, several steps would be required to complete the project, including: (1) the location of its music among the manuscripts in use at the time of the event, (2) the preparation of an edition of that music that would preserve its historical integrity while making it accessible to modern readers, (3) the assembling of documentary material from the Moravian records that describes the particular event and places it within its historical context, and (4) the presentation of the musical restoration and its interpretation in a complementary fashion.

This book is a result of the first effort at such a musical restoration. The event is the Day of Solemn Thanksgiving, the Fourth of July, 1783, as it was celebrated in Salem, North Carolina, to mark the end of the Revolutionary War. As a restored historical building loses much of its significance if it is moved from its original location, so the value of the restored musical event is lessened if it is separated from its surroundings. Therefore, as prelude to the Day of Solemn Thanksgiving, this volume includes a brief explanation of those musical traditions of the Moravian Church that pertain to the celebration held in Salem, together with a survey of musical activity in Salem prior to that Fourth of July. In this preliminary material, the archival documents tell the story. The principal sources of the numerous quotations consist of the diaries of the Moravian congregations and the minutes of meetings held by the governing boards of the community during the period under study. Since the various governing boards are mentioned frequently in the course of this book, their titles and duties are given here:

Aeltesten Conferenz (Elders Conference)—the board that governed the spiritual affairs of the community.

Aufseher Collegium (Board of Overseers)—the board that supervised the material and financial affairs of the town.

Gemeinrath (Congregation Council)—all adult members of the congregation, charged with making decisions of a civic nature.

Helfer Conferenz or *Grosse Helfer Conferenz*—an unofficial body of representatives from the governing boards listed above, together with several elected and ex officio members, who advised the boards on matters requiring official action.

The original documents are preserved in the Moravian Archives in Winston-Salem, North Carolina. Translated extracts from those documents are being published in *Records of the Moravians in North Carolina* (Raleigh, North Carolina, 1922–); other unpublished translations prepared by Erika Huber and Edmund Schwarze under the auspices of Old Salem, Incorporated, are filed in the Moravian Archives. The first four volumes of the published *Records*, containing translations by Adelaide L. Fries, and the unpublished translations of Huber and Schwarze have been of invaluable assistance in this project.

The completion of this study was made possible by two research grants awarded by The Florida State University. During the course of research and writing, several institutions and many individuals contributed information, time, effort, and moral support. I am especially grateful to Mary Creech, archivist of the Moravian Archives, Southern Province, Winston-Salem, North Carolina; Vernon Nelson, archivist of the Moravian Archives, Northern Province, Bethlehem, Pennsylvania; the Right Reverend Kenneth G. Hamilton, bishop of the Moravian Church; Karl Kroeger, director, and the staff and trustees of The Moravian Music Foundation, Incorporated; and Dean Wiley L. Housewright and Assistant Dean Joseph A. White of The Florida State University School of Music.

A special debt of gratitude is owed to the remarkable Miss Lily Peter of Marvell, Arkansas—a descendant of the hero of this study, Johann Friedrich Peter—whose unwavering support and enthusiasm for all phases of Moravian music research has contributed immeasurably to the successful completion of many projects. Finally, to my friends and colleagues, Frances Griffin, director of information at Old Salem, Incorporated, and Nicholas Bragg, former director of education at Old Salem and currently director of Reynolda House in Winston-Salem, North Carolina, and to my son, Stephen Gombosi, all of whom endured the sufferings and shared the celebrations, I extend my deepest appreciation for their patience and encouragement.

*A DAY
OF SOLEMN
THANKSGIVING*

I
The Moravian Church and Its Music

Any study of Moravian music must take into account those customs and practices of the Moravian Church that affect its music, for the two are so closely bound together that the music cannot be viewed separately without distorting its meaning and function.

The Moravian Church traces its origins back to the year 1457 when a group of religious dissidents, followers of the teachings of Jan Hus, gathered at Lititz, in what is now Czechoslovakia, to form a society known as the Unitas Fratrum, or the Unity of Brethren. From the Unity of Brethren came the first Protestant hymnal (1501) and numerous hymn collections in Czech, Polish, and German that continued to issue from its outlawed printing press during the Counter-Reformation. Extant copies of these hymnals furnish the only remaining documentation of the musical traditions of the Ancient Unity, but their presence is sufficient to show that, from its beginnings, the Unity appreciated the important role that music can play in spreading ideas and beliefs.

In the early eighteenth century, these Bohemian Brethren found asylum in Saxony, settling on the estate of Count Nicholas Ludwig von Zinzendorf (1700–1760), a devout Lutheran who assumed the leadership of the Unity. It was during this time that the group became known as the "Moravians," although the society retained its original name, or the German equivalent, *Brüdergemeine*. On Zinzendorf's estate near Berthelsdorf, the Moravians built the village of Herrnhut (then spelled Herrnhuth), which was to serve well into the nineteenth century as the controlling center of the Renewed Moravian Church. Herrnhut became a thriving, self-contained community, admitting as residents only those individuals who were willing to accept the regulation of their spiritual and secular lives by the codes of conduct set forth in the Brotherly Agreement adopted in 1727. The spiritual and material success of the Herrnhut experiment led the Moravians to continue the same pattern of government in congregation towns they later established in Europe and America.[1]

During the early years of the Renewed Moravian Church, the basic customs and traditions, many of which affect this study, were established.[2] Of primary importance was the decision to maintain a church archives. In each Moravian settlement, minutes were kept of all meetings of the governing boards and an official diary recorded the day-to-day happenings in the town; important events were singled out for lengthy and detailed description in special supplements (*Beilagen* or *Beylagen*) to the diary. Scattered among these records are many references to musical matters that must be pieced together to form a picture of musical life in the congregation town. At the end of each year, a Memorabilia was compiled, summarizing the year's activities. Copies of the Memorabilia and extracts from the diary were sent to the other Moravian congregations and to the church headquarters in Herrnhut so that the most widely separated communities remained in touch with one another and close ties were maintained with the governing center in Herrnhut.

Another means of maintaining those ties was the annual publication of Daily Text Books for use in all the congregations. For each day of the coming year, a passage from the Old Testament was drawn from a collection of scriptural verses stored in Herrnhut for the purpose. This passage, the *Loosung* or *Losung* (watchword), was coupled with a second biblical passage, the *Lehrtext* (text), chosen from the New Testament, and to each of the prescribed scriptural texts was attached an appropriate hymn verse. The resulting collection of Daily Texts was printed and disseminated among the various congregations for use in the following year. The Daily Texts are important in the musical history of the Moravians because they were often supplied with musical settings for performance on the appropriate day.

Among other practices of the eighteenth-century Moravians was the institution of the "Choir" system, i.e., the division of the congregation into groups according to age, sex, and marital status. In reading the German records it is important to keep in mind the fact that the term *Chor* refers to one of these groups: Single Sisters, Single Brothers, Married People, Widows, Widowers, Children, Older Boys, and Older Girls. A choir of musicians is indicated by such terms as *Choro musico*, *Chorus musicus*, *Sängerchor*, or *Posaunenchor*.

Encouraged by Count Zinzendorf, a prolific hymn writer with over two thousand hymns to his credit, the Moravians in Herrnhut continued the strong hymn tradition of the Ancient Unity and developed the musical liturgies. Several hymnals were published under Zinzendorf's direction but, although tunes were designated for the hymn texts, a printed choralebook did not appear until 1784. After Zinzendorf's death in 1760, the Moravians undertook to revise the hymnody of the church in order to eliminate some of the excessive emotionalism that the majority of the membership found distasteful, and within a few years, they could point with pride to their musical accomplishments. Full and informative descriptions of the musical practices of the church are included in Bishop August Gottlieb Spangenberg's authoritative account of the organizational structure and schedule of worship services followed by eighteenth-century Moravians.[3] Published in Germany in 1774, Spangenberg's book soon reached Salem, North Carolina, where, in 1778, the prominent merchant and civic leader, Traugott Bagge, completed its English translation for use in explaining Moravian customs and beliefs to visitors to the community who did not understand the German language.[4] In Bagge's translation, the Moravians' pride in the high quality of their hymnody and congregational singing is clearly evident:

There is something agreeable in the singing in the Brethren's meetings, because it is very distant from the otherwise customary loud bawling of the hymns, & thereby becomes the more devout & harmonious.

The hymns which are in use at present are mostly contained in the small Brethren's hymn-book, and are taken partly out of the ancient pithy hymns of the Unity of the Brethren & the protestant Lutheran Church, partly out of the Collections of Paul Gerhard & other new Hymnologists. The hymns which about 25 years ago came in vogue in the Congregation, and which certainly were not meant as partly by way of derision, partly thro' Misunderstanding they have been interpreted, yet also were not according to the measure of Simplicity and gravity becoming the divine Truth, and were mixed with all

sorts of play of words bordering upon dandling, are put out of all use long since.

Yea the Teachers in the Brethren's Church have taken all possible pains, from time to time, to express themselves also in hymns more inteligibly, pure and simple, & to word them in such language that a devoutly considering heart, in the use thereof, need not stop short or perhaps be silenced quite at the question: Understandest thou what thou singest?[5]

The liturgies of the church are described in this manner:

Towards 5 o'clock [on Sundays] there is a liturgical meeting of the Communicants, when a solemn hymn to the Father, Son and Holy Ghost is sung in fellowship.[6] . . . Besides the before-mentioned liturgical Meeting on Sundays there is also some Meetings held in the other Days of the week for singing such hymns of praise and thanksgiving. Among these the hymn: *O Head so full of bruises*, which is sung on Friday evenings, has its distinguishing Signature. At these liturgical Meetings the Kiss of Peace is imparted by everyone to him or her that stands close by, both on the Brethrens side and on the Sisters side,[7] at such words of the hymn as have a reference to the Covenant of Love and peace of the Congregation one among the other.

In singing these liturgical hymns the Brethren & Sisters sing by turns, some lines being sung by the former, others by the latter, & others again by both together, whereby the singing is made more agreeable, & the presence of mind is promoted.[8]

Antiphonal singing of chorales is also mentioned in the preface to the first printed choralebook published by the Moravians in 1784. Its compiler, Christian Gregor (1732–1801), not only recommends the alternation of succeeding lines of a chorale but also suggests that, in certain chorales, lines may be repeated antiphonally to good effect.[9] The choralebook and its companion, the new official hymnal of the Moravians, *Gesangbuch zum Gebrauch der evangelischen Brüdergemeinen* (Barby, 1778), were the result of the effort initiated by the Moravians twenty years earlier to revise and standardize the hymnody of the church. Charged with the task of organizing the music of the church was Bishop Christian Gregor, a member of the Unity Elders Conference and the most influential figure in the musical development of the Moravian Church. Gregor's musical interests went beyond hymn singing; he saw the need to develop an art-music tradition within the church as well. According to his autobiography,[10] he began the systematic development of that tradition in 1759 by composing or adapting preexistent music for voices and orchestra. These concerted anthems were performed during worship services held on special occasions and on festival days of the church.[11] While there are some single anthems among Gregor's compositions, the majority of his works are extended compositions consisting of several movements that the Moravians called Psalms or Cantatas in the eighteenth century, but which are commonly referred to today as Odes. Traugott Bagge translated Bishop Spangenberg's description of eighteenth-century Moravian art-music as follows:

For the festivals of the Christian Church in general, and for the festal memorial days peculiar to the Brethren's Church, some Psalms and Cantatas have been composed and printed from time to time.[12] These are performed by a musical choir in each Congregation, with gentle Music on Instruments, & the Congregation accompanies the same with singing at Intervalls Choruses [chorales] suitable to the matter.[13]

Texts for the Psalms or Cantatas were compiled from biblical passages and hymns and, often, original verses composed specifically for the day to be commemorated; the Daily Text and its accompanying hymn were often included within the Psalm text. Copies of the complete text were distributed to the congregation so that they could join in singing the chorales. Gregor's musical settings of the Psalms consist of recitatives, arias, duets, and choruses with instrumental accompaniment along with the chorales designed for congregational participation. Other Moravian composers, notably Johann Christian Geisler (1729–1815) and Johannes Herbst (1735–1812), followed Gregor's practice of compiling complete Psalms for specific occasions,[14] but younger musicians—at least in America—tended to compose single compositions. Psalms were still performed, but the musical directors in each settlement relied on the existing choral repertory to provide settings of the Psalm texts.

The Psalms or Cantatas, the most elaborate musical programs presented in any of the congregation meetings, were performed at a special gathering of the congregation, usually held in the afternoon of the day to be commemorated. This meeting, known as the Lovefeast (*Liebesmahl*)—not to be confused with Holy Communion (*Abendmahl*)—is characterized by the sharing of simple food, perhaps a sweet bun and coffee or tea, during the performance of the Psalm. The Moravians particularly enjoyed the spirit of fellowship that pervaded the Lovefeast and the music added pleasure to the occasion.

The Lovefeasts and liturgical meetings are but two of the numerous services the Moravians held on Sundays and weekdays. Two other gatherings, the Sunday Preaching Service and the *Singstunde*, are also of significance to this study. The Preaching Service, which, on special commemoration days, could be held on weekdays as well as on Sundays, began with congregational singing. Following the sermon, which was usually based on one of the day's prescribed texts, the service closed with prayer, the performance of an anthem by the choir and orchestra or a chorale by the congregation, and the Benediction. During the week, after work was ended, the Moravians gathered before bedtime for a *Singstunde*.[15] Matters of interest to the congregation might be discussed during these meetings and the Daily Texts were studied. The singing of chorales, however, was the main feature of the *Singstunde* and it was not unusual to use the occasion to learn new hymns. If guests were present, the choir and orchestra often performed special music during the *Singstunde*.

To support its musical program, each Moravian settlement maintained a brass choir (*Posaunenchor*) and an orchestra in addition to the choir. The study of music was encouraged from childhood through maturity so that each town was assured of the services of organists, instrumentalists, and singers. Every community maintained a library of musical parts and a collection of instruments that was augmented by privately owned instruments. With these resources, the Moravians were equipped to meet the musical needs of the church and community.

This, then, was the heritage of the Moravians who were chosen to establish colonies in America during the eighteenth century. The cherished customs and traditions—the Lovefeasts, *Singstunden*, and Preaching Services; the liturgies and hymns, the more elaborate concerted music for worship services and special observances; the musical organizations and educational system that provided for the training of composers and performers; the instrument collections and music libraries; the sense of order and history manifested in the keeping and preserving of records—all were transplanted to the New World.

PLATE 1. *Proclamation by Governor Alexander Martin, 18 June 1783.*
By permission of the Moravian Archives, Southern Province, Winston-Salem, North Carolina. Courtesy of Old Salem, Incorporated.

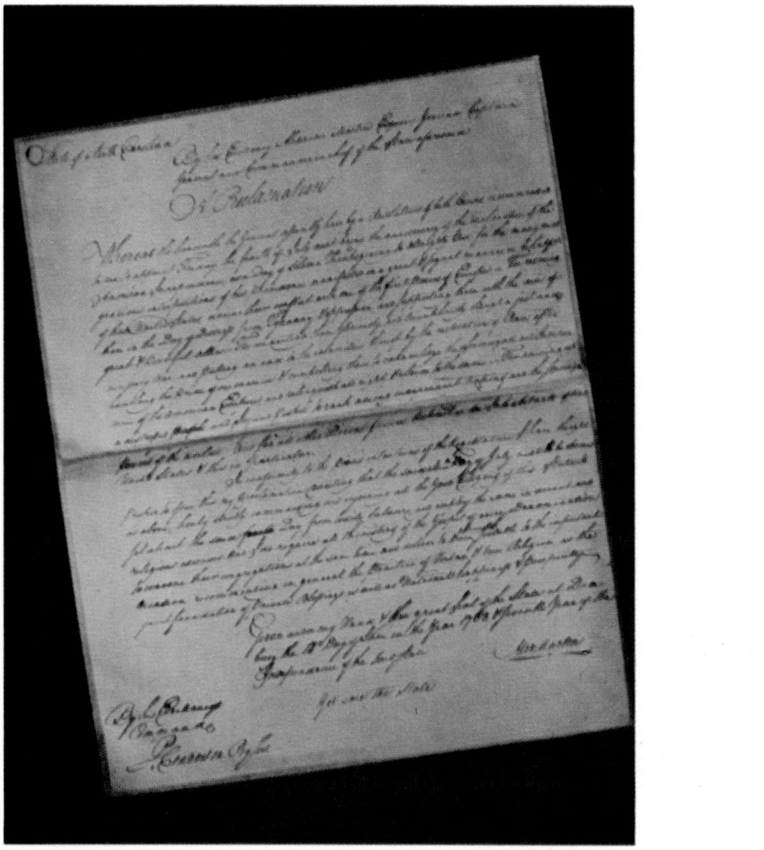

PLATE 2. *Salem* Gemeinhaus, *painting by Stuart Archibald.*
By permission of Salem College, Winston-Salem, North Carolina. Courtesy of Old Salem, Incorporated.

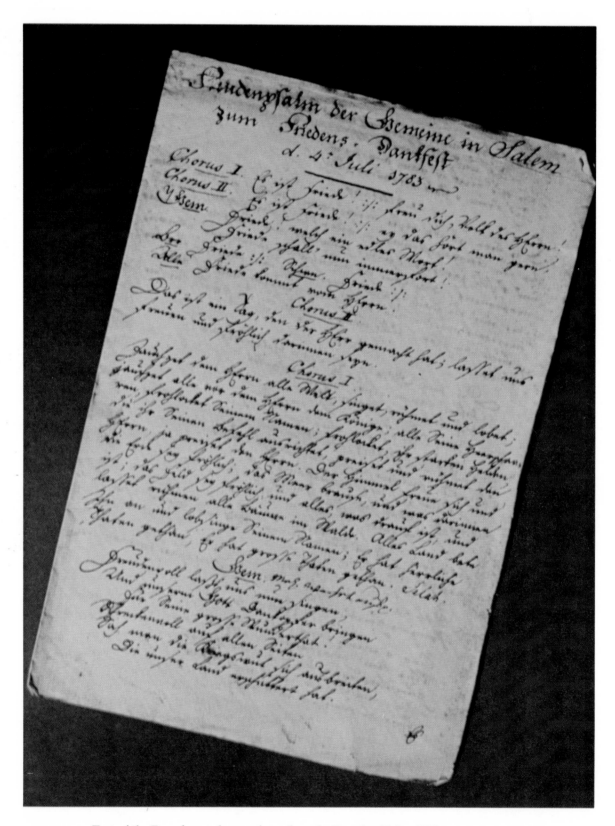

PLATE 3. *Text of the* Freudenpsalm, *performed on the Fourth of July, 1783,*
in Salem, North Carolina, preserved at The Moravian Music Foundation,
Winston-Salem, North Carolina.
Courtesy of Old Salem, Incorporated.

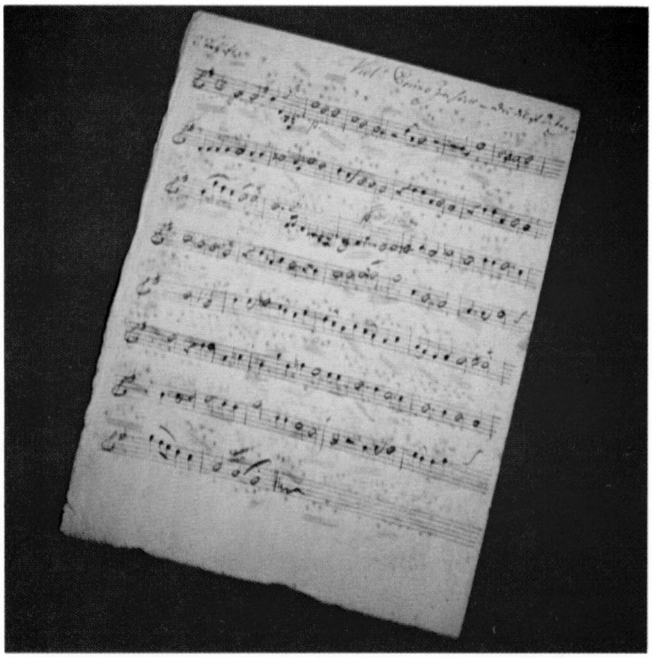

PLATE 4. *"Das ist ein Tag," Organo part dated 1780, "old"*
No. 53, preserved at The Moravian Music Foundation,
Winston-Salem, North Carolina.
Courtesy of Old Salem, Incorporated.

PLATE 5. *"Das ist ein Tag," violin part with cue*
marking, preserved at The Moravian Music Foundation,
Winston-Salem, North Carolina.
Courtesy of Old Salem, Incorporated.

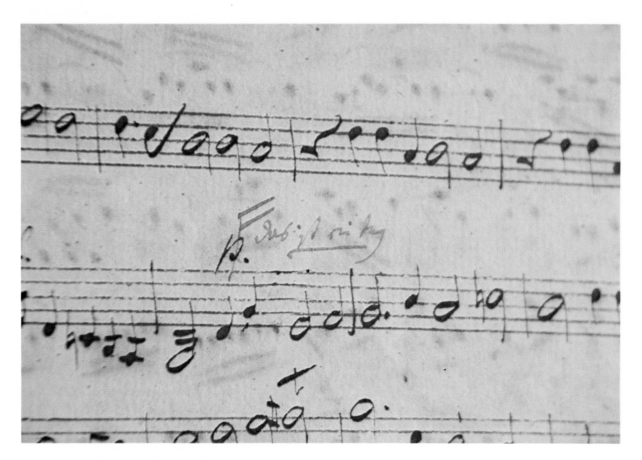

PLATE 6. *"Das ist ein Tag," violin part, close-up of cue marking.*
Courtesy of Old Salem, Incorporated.

PLATE 7. *Partbook containing chorales, used by Salem musicians in the 1780s, preserved at The Moravian Music Foundation, Winston-Salem, North Carolina. Courtesy of Old Salem, Incorporated.*

Music in Salem Prior to the Fourth of July, 1783

After an unsuccessful attempt to settle in Georgia (1735), the Moravians turned to Pennsylvania, establishing a primary center in Bethlehem (1741) and other congregation towns including Lititz and Nazareth. The Unity wished to expand its missionary work southward and so, when Lord Granville offered to sell the Moravians 100,000 acres of land in North Carolina, a surveying party was sent to select the site for new settlements. Led by Bishop August Gottlieb Spangenberg,[1] head of the Unity in America, the party set out from Bethlehem, Pennsylvania, on 25 August 1752 and spent almost five months tramping through the Granville properties, staking out various tracts of land for the Moravians to purchase.

On 8 January 1753 Spangenberg recorded in his travel diary: *"From the camp in the three forks of Muddy Creek . . . The land on which we are now encamped seems to me to have been reserved by the Lord for the Brethren."*[2] Comprising approximately 73,000 acres, this tract of land in the three forks of Muddy Creek was named "Wachovia" (*die Wachau*) by Spangenberg after the region in Austria that had been the original homeland of the Zinzendorf family. Wachovia in North Carolina was destined to become the homeland of the Moravians who settled in the southern part of America.

By October 1753 the purchase of the North Carolina lands was completed and the Moravians were ready to begin the building of Wachovia. The church Elders decided that a preliminary town in Wachovia, to be called "Bethabara," would be established from which the building of the permanent Moravian center in North Carolina could be carried on. On 7 October 1753 the Pennsylvania Moravians gathered in Bethlehem to fete the fifteen Single Brothers[3] who were to make the initial journey to North Carolina and, of course, the main event of the celebration was a *Singstunde*.[4] As the journey began with music, so it ended on Saturday, 17 November, with a Lovefeast and the singing of a special verse composed by one of the party for the occasion:

We hold arrival Lovefeast here,
  In Carolina land,
A company of Brethren true,
  A little Pilgrim Band,
Called by the Lord to be of those
  Who through the whole world go,
To bear Him witness everywhere,
  And naught but Jesus know.[5]

After a day of rest, the Brethren set to work sharpening tools, bringing in food supplies, building a bake oven, measuring off the first land to be cleared, laying the floor of the first cabin, building a cooper's bench and wash trough, setting up a grindstone—and, at the end of that first day's labors, holding a *Singstunde*.[6] With such a beginning, it is not surprising to learn that music accompanied every step in the building of Wachovia.

The first colonists were preoccupied with surviving in the wilderness and establishing the town of Bethabara to prepare the way for the settlers to follow, but the church diary of that first year in Wachovia records the fact that time was found to hold Lovefeasts and *Singstunden*. There is little specific information concerning the music used during those meetings or its manner of performance, but hymnbooks and hymn singing are mentioned frequently.

The earliest mention of musical instruments in Wachovia appears about three months after the colonists' arrival in Bethabara when, on 23 February 1754, the diarist wrote with considerable pride that "Lovefeast was announced with our new trumpet, which we made from a hollow tree, and no trumpet in Bethlehem has a better tone [!]"[7] By the end of the year 1755, the prized wooden trumpet was joined, and perhaps replaced, by other trumpets[8] as well as horns[9] and flutes.[10] Two violins[11] were added to the group during the following year, and on 24 December 1756 eight musicians with their instruments led the congregational singing during the Christmas Eve Watch Meeting.[12]

With the acquisition of an organ in 1762, the musical activity in Bethabara gained new impetus. Brought from Bethlehem by a party of colonists including Johann Michael Graff who was to serve later as pastor, archivist, and musical director in Salem, the new organ was first used on 8 July 1762: "Bro. Graff set up in our *Saal* the organ he brought from Bethlehem;[13] and during the *Singstunde* in the evening we heard an organ played for the first time in Carolina, and were very happy and grateful that it had reached us safely."[14]

The Bethabara Congregation owned seven instruments at the time the first extant inventory was taken on 14 August 1766. That inventory (*Inventarium der Mobillien u. Instrumente im Gemein Haus*[15] *Bethabara d. 14. Aug. 1766*)[16] lists the following instruments "zu Liturgischem Gebraucs" ("for liturgical use"):

1 Orgel (organ)
1 Pass Geige (violoncello)
1 Violin
2 Trompeten (trumpets)
2 Wald Hörner mit Krum Bogen und aufsietze
(natural horns with crooks and mouthpieces)

The instruments listed above represent only those that were owned by the congregation as a whole; in addition, there were privately owned instruments that were not included in the inventory. The precise number and kind of instruments owned by individual citizens of the community cannot be determined, but their existence may be inferred from such casual statements found in the records as: "Br. Graff was asked to take his flute along, and he played while the little Abraham Transow sang several verses"[17] or "In the estate of Brother Bonn there is a violin which has been used in the Service up to now. We shall consider who can buy it because we cannot spare the instrument in our music."[18] In 1768 the Wachovia Moravians received their first set of trombones (treble, alto, tenor, and bass), the instruments that played a primary role in their congregation music. Their arrival was singled out for special mention in the Memorabilia for that year: "During the year we have received from Europe a set of trombones, and their use on solemn days and festivals has strengthened and edified our congregation."[19]

The Moravian records for the early years in Wachovia often mention the playing of instruments to welcome visitors to the community and the singing of hymns and original verses during Lovefeasts and *Singstunden*, but descriptions of other musical activities are difficult to find. Only in the account of Governor Tryon's visit is there a fuller explanation of music's role in community life:[20]

[Friday, 18 September 1767] They were welcomed with music on the trumpets and French Horns. . . . Half an hour later dinner was served to all of them in the *Saal* in the Brothers' House. The meal was accompanied by music, and pleased them very much.

[Sunday, 20 September 1767] In the morning the English minister preached. . . . All had to go quietly today, no music being used. In the afternoon, however, the Governor's Lady went alone into our *Saal*, and played a little on the organ, our girls came in and began to sing, which pleased the Lady so much that Br. Graff must play for them; then the Governor also came, and they entertained themselves in this way most happily for a whole hour, the Lady being particularly pleased. She visited the girls in their own room, then had them come again to the *Saal* to sing for her, this time in German—she had the English Hymn Book and wanted the verses they were singing pointed out to her. She must, against her inclination, leave them for tea. . . . Br. Graff held the *Gemeinstunde* . . . attended by all the distinguished guests . . . the responsive singing [of the Liturgy] by the various choirs especially appealed to the Governor. . . . At bedtime the musicians played softly before the house.

It is from this account that we learn that the Wachovians used music for entertainment purposes—even dinner music and serenades—as well as for worship and that they followed the Moravian practice of antiphonal singing in their hymns and liturgies.

A later visit by Governor Tryon, although it took place under less pleasant circumstances, provides a few more details of musical life in Wachovia. Accompanied this time by his army and several prisoners taken during skirmishes with the Regulators, the governor arrived in Bethabara on 4 June 1771. The musical entertainments held during his first visit must have lingered in the governor's memory for "in the evening the Governor came to the *Singstunde*, having let it be known in advance that he wished to hear the beautiful singing of the Sisters."[21] The following morning, on their way to hold maneuvers in a field outside Bethabara, the governor's army marched through the town, "our musicians leading and playing on the trombones and violins."[22] At dinner that day, celebrating the birthday of King George III, "several Healths were drunk, each being answered with a loud *Hurra* and the playing of a verse on the trombones by our musicians."[23]

The story of the North Carolina Moravians and their music has focused thus far on Bethabara, the first settlement and the base from which the Moravians intended to carry on the building of Salem, the central town. Trades and professions were to be moved to Salem while Bethabara reverted to an agricultural community. Though reluctant to tamper with the prosperous growth of Bethabara, the Moravians followed the directive of the Unity Elders and began to turn their attention to Salem. The specific location of the new town[24] was determined on 14 February 1765,[25] and on 6 January 1766 "a dozen Brethren . . . took a wagon and went to the new town site where . . . they cut down the trees on the place where the first house was to stand, singing several stanzas as they worked."[26]

The building of Salem occupied the Moravians for the next five years. Every step in its construction—the location and the design of each building—had been carefully planned and was just as carefully executed. With the completion of the *Gemeinhaus* in November 1771,[27] the Salem Congregation was organized and the transferral of church affairs, trades, and population began. The building was consecrated on 13 November 1771 in the presence of all the Wachovia Moravians and three representatives of the Unity Elders Conference from Herrnhut who were special guests for the occasion; one of those representatives was Christian Gregor, the man who shaped the musical character of the Renewed Moravian Church. At the noon Lovefeast, held in the new *Saal* of the *Gemeinhaus* and attended by more than three hundred persons, a Festal Psalm was sung by soloists, choir, and congregation.[28] The *Saal* was to be the scene of many such musical events held during special observances, including the Day of

Solemn Thanksgiving celebrated on the Fourth of July, 1783, for it served as the place of worship for the Salem Congregation until the present church edifice was built at the turn of the nineteenth century. The first musical program was hampered, however, by the lack of instrumentalists and an organ.

A proper organ for the *Saal* had been under discussion even before the cornerstone for the *Gemeinhaus* was laid. In their meeting on 20 June 1769 the Elders Conference discussed the possibility of ordering an instrument to be built in Lititz, Pennsylvania, by the Moravian organ builder, David Tannenberg,[29] but when Tannenberg's price of £200 was learned, the Elders rightly feared that the high cost would be objectionable to the Salem Congregation.[30] They turned next to Joseph Ferdinand Bullitschek,[31] a Bohemian cabinetmaker,[32] coffin maker,[33] and millwright[34] who had recently settled in Bethania, a village lying just outside Bethabara. Bullitschek first submitted a sketch for an organ containing three ranks, at an estimated cost of £70.[35] The Salem Elders countered with a proposal that he build a smaller one-stop instrument;[36] a compromise was reached on 4 February 1772:

We have spoken with Br. Bullitschek. . . . He makes the following proposition:

a. To make an organ like the one in Bethabara.[37] For this he asks £26 N.C.

b. If he would arrange the windchest and bellows so that another stop in the Bass register could be added later (that stop, of course to be paid for later) he would charge £30. If one or more additions would have to be made to take care of future expansion, the cost might possibly be £32.

Conference approved "b." He promises to deliver the organ by the beginning or middle of May. At Br. Enerson's there is a good supply of dry walnut wood. One could give Br. Bullitschek a quantity of this in lieu of the first payment on the organ.[38]

When the May deadline approached, the organ was not finished as promised and Bullitschek demanded more money from the Moravians. At a meeting of the *Helfer Conferenz* on 4 May 1772 it "was agreed that Br. Bullitschek shall receive ten pounds more than the 32 pounds called for in the contract, since he is making it with two stops."[39] Finally, in October: "Br. Bullitschek set up our new organ and tuned it with Br. Graff's help. When finished it was immediately played for services and will make them, and especially the *Singstunde*, more attractive."[40]

In a report to the Unity Elders Conference, F. W. Marshall, minister and business manager of the Salem Congregation, wrote this description of the new organ: "It has two stops, is neatly made, has a very good tone, the organist can see the minister through it, and in general it is as well arranged as we could wish."[41] Marshall's remark that "the organist can see the minister through it" refers to the fact that the construction and placement of the organ was such that the organist sat with his back to the rear wall of the *Saal* and faced the attached console. Had not Bullitschek devised the ingenious solution in the form of a window cut through the organ case immediately above the music rack, the organist would have had no visual contact with the minister or congregation during services,[42] a situation that would impede the orderly conduct of the various orders of worship. The Memorabilia for 1772 mentions the gratitude of the congregation for the opportunity to "attend the liturgies and other services in our new *Gemein Saal* (services rendered more pleasing and brighter by the new organ)."[43] While the Salem citizens were delighted at first with their new organ, they soon began to find fault with it and its builder; some of their complaints will be reviewed later, but one document dating from 1774 deserves mention here. In an undated memorandum from the *Helfer Conferenz* to the Congregation Council,[44] attention is drawn to the fact that "Bullitschek stays in Salem at the moment, and we shall have him tune our new organ. Also a few new pipes must be installed. Br. Tiersch[45] has agreed to put in the four new pipes which he brought with him and to tune the organ. . . . He [Bullitschek] is not to accept any other work before our organ is finished. The repairs will take only a few days." From the tone of the memorandum, it can be inferred that the church officials were becoming impatient with the procrastinating Bullitschek who often failed to live up to agreements.

The acquisition of other instruments for Salem did not encounter as many obstacles as the purchase of

the organ. On 24 January 1772, scarcely two months after the congregation was organized, the Salem diarist wrote that "our Choir of Musicians played here for the first time, accompanying the singing of *Haupt voll Blut und Wunden*."[46] The following month, on 16 February, representatives from Salem, Bethabara, and Bethania met in Bethabara to decide which of the communally owned instruments then in Bethabara should be transferred to Salem for "use in the *Saal* and at Lovefeasts,"[47] and on 28 September 1772 a report was made to the *Aufseher Collegium* that an inventory of the instruments transferred to Salem had been made. The Collegium noted that "it would be well to have a separate closet made for the instruments in the Brothers' House. When repairs are needed, the head of the Congregation fund should be consulted. The musicians are requested to be careful with the instruments, even though no one has been expressly charged with it."[48]

The 1772 inventory of instruments could shed considerable light on the composition of the "Choir of Musicians" mentioned by the diarist, but, unfortunately, no trace of the inventory has been found in either the Salem archives or in the collection of musical documents housed in The Moravian Music Foundation. However, from entries in the financial accounts, minutes of the various governing boards, and from descriptions given in the Salem Diary of music performed during the 1770s, it is clear that Salem possessed at that time a full complement of instruments, i.e., trumpets, horns, trombones, flutes, and strings (Figure A) as well as the organ (Figure B) and that the town musicians carried on the usual functions associated with Moravian communities, escorting guests, announcing deaths, and performing at Lovefeasts and *Singstunden*.

Funds to sustain the musical activities were obtained from the Congregation Fund,[49] donations from the various Choirs of the congregation,[50] and, when necessary, from special collections; the latter were often taken at the close of the year, but, if the need was pressing, they could be scheduled at any time. Contributions from the visitors to the community also helped to defray expenses: "Br. Reuter showed an account that the Choir of musicians were in debt five pounds for violin strings. For the payment of

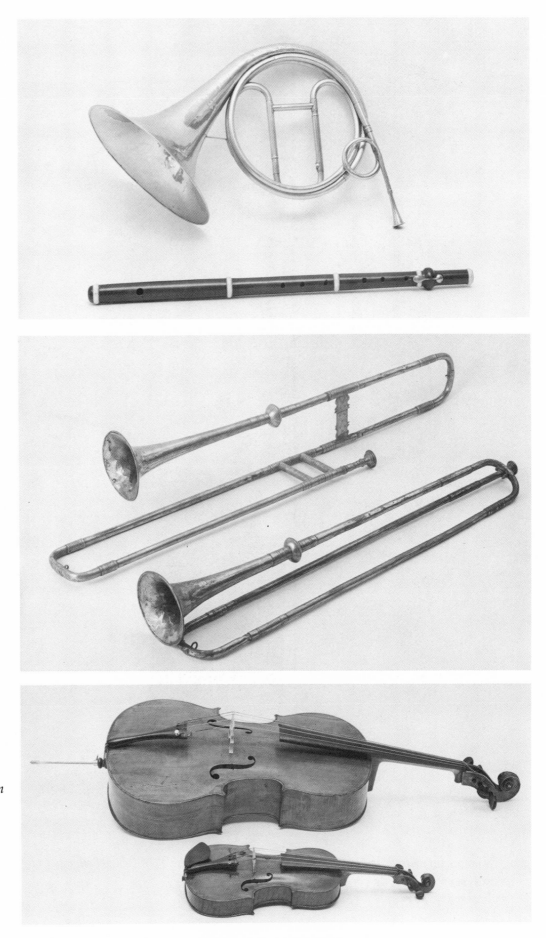

FIGURE A. *Instruments used by the Salem Moravians in the eighteenth century, preserved in the Wachovia Museum, Winston-Salem, North Carolina.*
Courtesy of Old Salem, Incorporated.

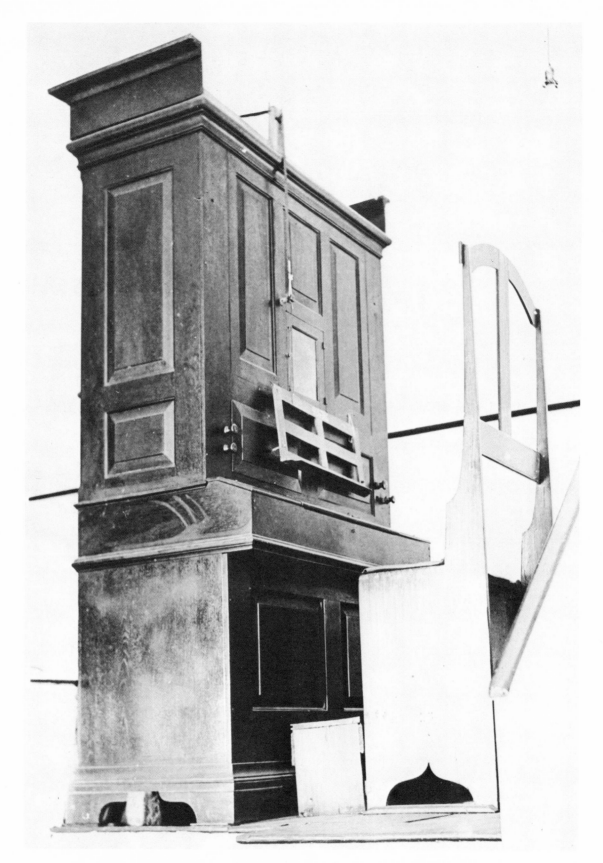

FIGURE B. *Organ built by Joseph Ferdinand Bullitschek in 1773 for the Bethania Congregation, a twin of the Salem Bullitschek organ (1772).*
Courtesy of Old Salem, Incorporated.

this, the suggestion was made to take up a special offering at one of the *public* [italics added] services, announcement to be made beforehand."[51] This collection netted but £3/16/10, so "it was decided to put the -/23/2 in the Poor Account to it, considering the fact that they [the poor] often get something into their account from visitors because of the music."[52] When the *Saal* was first put into use, two collection boxes had been fashioned to hold contributions for the poor,[53] and later, in 1775, it was "proposed that the contribution boxes in the *Saal* be painted in order that they might more readily catch the eyes of visitors who come to see the *Saal* and the organ."[54]

The care given to the musical affairs of the town resulted in a high quality of music that impressed visitors to the community. In a letter of appreciation written to his hosts,[55] a former member of the King's Council in North Carolina, a Samuel Strudwick, included this assessment of the congregation music:

When I was present at your Evening Meetings the solemn, sober stile of your Music seem'd admirably adapted to inspire a temperate & rational Devotion. Far from exciting the passions & transporting the mind with Extasies which do violence to the human frame, leaving Reason at a distance, and soaring into the Region of Fancy and wild Enthusiasm, It is calculated to attune & harmonize the Passions, to calm all the perturbations of the Mind, to dispose it to meditate on the high priviledge of Christianity, and sooth it into a tranquil and serene Joy. In your Love Feasts you indulge more the power of Harmony, tho' not to Excess: I felt myself there more Elevated & Warm'd but with a gentle heat that imparted Gladness, Charity and Benevolence.[56]

The town leaders kept a constant eye on the musical activities in Salem, and they were quick to stifle any unseemly conduct on the part of the musicians. "It should not be permissible that the musicians play minuets, polonaises, marches and all secular music of that kind [on Sunday]. They should play chorales. We also think and want to remind everyone that not every young man learns to play an instrument whenever he pleases, because many have thus come to a bad way of life and have neglected their real profession."[57] The study of music, however, was encouraged and valued by the Salem officials. In devising the curriculum for the Boys' School, they determined that "reading, writing, and arithmetic are the foundation studies; geography, *music* [italics added], geometry, and speaking are of the next importance.[58] . . . A hymn shall be sung at the opening and close of school, both rooms uniting;[59] in this way the boys will learn to sing better."[60]

Musical training was not confined to the schoolroom, nor was it limited to any age-group. "When the [preschool] children have had some practice in singing, they shall have a short song service [*Singstunde*] once a week, or a liturgy that is partly singing. . . . When Br. Reuz has married, he shall teach singing to the Sisters [adult women]."[61] That the musical situation in the community was of concern to its leaders is apparent in statements found in the minutes of board meetings, such as "we are beginning to be short of men who can play the French Horn, and will try to secure two boys who will learn."[62] Individuals possessing musical talent were encouraged to develop that talent for the enrichment of the community's musical life: "So that the two boys, Gottlieb Fockel and Jacob Meyer, may have practice in singing, they shall be used in the choir in singing the liturgy *O head so full of bruises*. Br. Peter will instruct them in singing; and he will give Br. Oesterlein lessons in organ-playing, so that Bethabara may have an organist."[63] The music instructor, "Br. Peter," was Johann Friedrich (or John Frederik) Peter[64] who arrived in Salem on 15 June 1780 to take over some official duties from the overworked Bishop Graff "on whom everything rested, including matters which it had not been the intention that he should handle."[65]

Shortly after his arrival in Salem, Friedrich Peter presented himself to the Elders Conference "and was heartily welcomed. . . . Br. Peter has given himself heart and soul to his Saviour's service and will serve the Congregation in many ways: in the *Saal* as Lector; in the Elders Conference as secretary; to help Brn. Marshall and Graff with their correspondence; to encourage the Congregation with his musical gifts and lead the young people in music."[66] Further duties and financial compensation were assigned to Peter by the *Aufseher Collegium*: "Br. Friedrich Peter, who is to write the Minutes for the congregation, copy the Diaries, and help in other ways, is granted a yearly salary of £40: good money, if this proves to be insufficient it shall be increased. The Diaconie shall pay his room rent, and he shall not be expected to contribute to the Congregation fund."[67] Immediately upon his assignment of duties, Peter began to demonstrate his dedication to service. Within six months, he organized a weekly singing school,[68] assumed responsibility for collecting donations to the music fund,[69] was ordained a deacon,[70] preached his first sermon in Salem,[71] and served Holy Communion for the first time.[72] With the beginning of the year 1781, he accepted yet another role as church diarist (a post relinquished to him by the aged Bishop Graff), thereby assuming responsibility for compiling and writing the official diary, the annual Memorabilia, and accounts of special events for the Salem Congregation.[73]

In the latter part of 1782, Peter was charged with keeping the church archives, which, for his convenience, were moved to his living quarters;[74] he served as archivist until 17 May 1785.[75] An additional assignment given to Peter at this time was the supervision of the Boys' School, which the Elders felt was in need of improvement: "Br. Peter will not only supervise the school but also teach those subjects in which Br. Joseph Dixon [the schoolmaster] is not well-versed."[76] Following the death of Bishop Graff on 29 August 1782, the congregation was without a preacher until 5 December of that year, when the Congregation Council announced that "Br. Peter will succeed the late Br. Graff as Preacher. There has been thought of marrying him, but when this plan was carefully considered in the Elders Conference,[77] it was decided that it would be better for him to remain single for the present. Since the entire community has been wondering about this matter, they will be informed of the decision by the Elders Conference so that they will not be left with uncertainty."[78] With the new post, Peter's responsibilities increased along with his income,[79] for he continued to carry on all of his previous duties except the collection of donations to the music fund, a task now assigned to Johannes Reuz.[80]

During the decade of his tenure in Salem, Peter so executed his responsibilities that the diarist, who succeeded him in that post, was moved to write on the eve of Peter's departure from Salem: "Br.

Friedrich Peter has served this Congregation faithfully for ten years, has taught in the school for little boys, has directed the music, has kept the minutes for the *Aeltesten Conferenz*, and has held services."[81] While he filled many posts in Salem, Peter's leadership in musical activities was, without doubt, his most outstanding contribution to the community. When it was learned that he was to be called to serve another congregation, the church officials immediately began to search for ways to fill the void that would be created by his absence. Excerpts from the minutes of the various meetings held during the time reveal the extent of Peter's influence on every phase of Salem's musical life:

[30 June 1790] Consideration was given to the matter of music as the call of Br. Friedrich Peter to another place leaves the Congregation without a director of music. In the first place, it is understood that the *Aeltesten Conferenz* prepares the odes and has all music matters under general supervision. To carry on the music and attend to all details connected with it, we knew no one to suggest but Br. Reuz. We hesitate to place the music and the instruments entirely in his hands, and agreed to have a closet made in which it can be placed in the small *Saal*, and Br. Reuz shall keep the key. Br. Peter shall give the music and a catalog of it to Br. Reuz, if he is willing to take charge of it.

In order that the daily services may have organ music, the Brethren who can play the organ, that is, Reuz, Schober, Seiz, and Meinung, shall be consulted next Sunday. Br. Bagge shall be asked whether he can and will give time to his son Benjamin to play the organ in the children's services.[82]

[3 July 1790] Br. Benzien has undertaken to prepare the odes for the congregational and church festivals.[83]

[6 July 1790] Br. Peter has kept, up to now, the instruments and other musical items. Since he is going to leave us soon, it will be best to deposit these things in the *Gemeinhaus*, and have a closet made for that purpose, which Br. Wagemann can take over, if he can get the help of Br. Beroth.[84]

[7 July 1790] Br. Reuz has undertaken the oversight of the music for one year. The Brn. Reuz, Schober, and Meinung will play the organ in turn, one week at a time.[85]

[14 July 1790] Br. Bagge . . . will be glad to have Benjamin [his son] used for the organplaying in the children's services.[86]

[19 August 1790] In the lower part of the music closet, there is a place for the violins, so the violin strings should also be kept there.[87]

The numerous details involved in the musical program, which for ten years had been only a part of Friedrich Peter's official duties, were now the concern of many men.

Immediately upon his arrival in 1780, Peter began to assess the musical conditions in Salem. But one week after his welcome by the town officials, he made his first plea to the *Aufseher Collegium* for musical supplies and funds, suggesting that a special collection for music be made "because we could buy strings now at a very good price from the store. However, since Br. [Traugott] Bagge [the store-keeper] has promised to keep as many strings as we need on hand, the collection was postponed."[88] Peter was not deterred by the board's inaction and he pursued the subject at subsequent meetings: "At Br. Peter's request, Br. Bagge mentioned the fact that the violin strings he has on hand are too coarse for the hot weather and that, if possible, he will get some that are finer. We all agreed that he should."[89] After four months, the board finally agreed that "it might be a good time to have a collection to buy strings for the musicians."[90] That freewill collection netted the musicians' fund "£5/4/11 and 45 Continental Dollars,"[91] an amount that not only covered the purchase of the strings and a music rack as well as the cost of repairs for some wind instruments, but also left a surplus of £1/11/- in the music account.[92]

The new year, 1781, saw increasing dissatisfaction with the Bullitschek organ (Figure B) and various complaints and proposed solutions concerning the instrument were offered during several board meetings:[93]

[19 April 1781] The musicians wish that a better tone could be given to the organ which shrieks aloud when facing the congregation.[94] We recently found that the tone was more pleasant when the organ was turned around, but it is not safe to have it back against the wall because of the moisture that gathers there, which would damage the organ. Br. Krause thinks he can box up the side toward the front [i.e., the back of the organ case that faced into the *Saal*], and can make a top which can be opened and closed at will. This will improve the tone and was approved.[95]

[31 May 1781] During the past few days . . . the tone of the organ has been improved by a box and swell.[96]

[19 July 1781] The swell mechanism on the organ should be fixed so that its creaking will not interfere with the congregation's devotions.[97]

An end to the creaking must have been made for there are no further references to the offending swell mechanism. Despite such minor annoyances, Friedrich Peter looked back with satisfaction upon the results of his first full year as music director, writing in the Wachovia Memorabilia that "the Congregation music in Salem has been improved this year, so that the hymns and liturgies on festal days have become brighter and more pleasing, and even strangers and travelers have been touched and will remember it. We thank the Lord for this treasure, and pray that He will preserve it to us, so that our singing may become constantly more liturgical and pleasing to Him."[98]

Several months of the year 1781 were devoted to preparing the community for an event that caused much apprehension among the citizens of Salem. The first inkling appears in the Salem Diary entry of 17 July 1781: "Several members of the [North Carolina] Assembly passed [through here] on their return to their homes. From them we learned that it had been decided to hold the next session here in Salem in November. May our dear Lord direct this according to His will, for he can turn the hearts of the mighty of this earth even as He turns the course of water-brooks."[99] Because of their refusal to bear arms, the Moravians endured much abuse and hardship during the war. Their willingness to pay the threefold tax for exemption from military service, to nurse the sick and wounded, and to supply shelter and provisions (sometimes without compensation) had earned the respect of men on both sides of the conflict. Yet there were some individuals who, not knowing the Moravians and their religious beliefs, were suspicious of the pacifist Brethren and even wished to deny them ownership of the Wachovia tract.[100] The meeting of the Assembly in Salem, therefore, was viewed by the Moravians as a time "during which the Saviour presented His people before the eyes of the world,"[101] and they made elaborate preparations for the session. "This will make many changes in our ordinary programs, but if with all modesty we hold to our chief purpose, if our conduct shows all people that we are children of God, and if we treat them in an orderly manner and with courtesy, then the Saviour will turn to good the evil that was intended us."[102]

The Moravians turned to their friend Alexander Martin,[103] the acting governor, to advise them in their preparations for the coming Assembly.[104] Acting upon his suggestions, provisions were gathered weeks before the arrival of the Assembly, extra bedding was brought from the outlying Moravian settlements, suitable lodgings were selected for the representatives, arrangements were made for stabling their horses, and the tradesmen were given instructions to follow in their dealings with the visiting dignitaries.[105] The church Elders also gave careful thought to the conduct of the musicians during the Assembly:

Musicians are to be reminded that they are not to play for the Assemblymen in private homes, saying that this is not our custom. . . . Violins are to be kept locked up in order not to be used for unfitting purposes; also the mouthpieces of the wind instruments.[106]

In our Congregation music, however, we will not be disturbed.[107] As long as there is no unusual disturbance, our week-day services shall be held in their usual order. The evening meal for the gentlemen of the Assembly comes just between our two services, and they can be informed that if they wish to attend our services, which will continue as usual, they may do so. This will be a pleasant way to avoid disorder.[108]

Of special concern to the Elders was the celebration of the tenth anniversary of the consecration of the *Gemeinhaus* and the *Saal*, which occurred while the Assembly was in Salem: "Concerning the solemn services for tomorrow [13 November], it was decided to hold the first meeting at 9 A.M., the Lovefeast at 3 P.M., and, at 8 P.M., the *Singstunde* with special instrumental music; the trombones will play during the first two services. All services will be open to the public; if the gentlemen of the Assembly wish to attend, they shall be welcome."[109] Friedrich Peter's report of the celebration in the church diary indicates that the Elders' plans were carried out successfully: "We celebrated the day with three public, solemn services, remembering the consecration of our *Saal*

ten years ago, and also joining with the entire Unity in thanking the Lord for his goodness as our Lord and Elder. At the Lovefeast, a psalm of thanksgiving was sung with instrumental accompaniment. In the evening service, hymns were sung and instrumental selections were rendered. The gentlemen of the Assembly attended the festal services with respect and reverence, and the Governor expressed his appreciation."[110]

During their stay in Salem, the assemblymen filled the *Saal* to capacity for the Preaching Services[111] and attended the *Singstunden* in even greater numbers, so that "our *Saal* could not hold the crowd that assembled . . . and many had to stay outside."[112] On the eve of their departure, the assemblymen were treated to "several selections with instrumental accompaniment for their pleasure."[113] Having thus enjoyed their visit, they decided to meet again in Salem early in the next year. For the second session, the Salem officials gave fewer instructions but "there was a reminder that the Brothers should take better care of the violins and other instruments so that the visitors in the community do not get the idea to use them in a manner that we would not like them to be used."[114]

The successful presentation of the Moravians before the "eyes of the world" during the two sessions of the Assembly was due in large part to the musical accomplishments of the Brethren, and the church officials were quick to give the musicians the credit they deserved. In describing the assemblymen's visit, F. W. Marshall wrote that "our music and singing had a great effect on them and they listened with wonder and respect. An old gray-haired gentleman came to me expressly before leaving and said that . . . if he could do anything for us in the Assembly, personally or by his influence, he would do it gladly."[115]

Though the Wachovia Moravians had some assurance of greater acceptance by their neighbors and safety from persecution as a result of friendships formed during the Assembly meetings in Salem, they still longed for an end to war and a return to the calm, orderly life of a Moravian congregation town. More than a year passed before word of that long-awaited peace reached the people of Salem.

III

A Day of Solemn Thanksgiving

On Great Sabbath (Holy Saturday), 19 April 1783, Friedrich Peter noted in the Salem Diary that "we found it remarkable that, on this day commemorating the Rest of our Lord in the Tomb, we learned that peace shall be restored to this land by the treaty drawn in Paris on January 20th of this year."[1] On the same day, Governor Alexander Martin announced the news to the North Carolina Assembly, which happened to be in session at the time; on 16 May just prior to adjournment, the Assembly instructed Governor Martin to proclaim the Fourth of July, 1783, as a day of general thanksgiving.[2] In compliance with the Assembly's wishes, Governor Martin issued the following proclamation (Plate 1):[3]

State of North Carolina:
By His Excellency Alexander Martin, Esquire,
Governor Captain-General and Commander-in-Chief
of the State aforesaid.

A PROCLAMATION

Whereas the honorable the General Assembly have by a Resolution of both Houses recommended to me to appoint the fourth of July next being the anniversary of the declaration of the American Independence, as a Day of Solemn Thanksgiving to Almighty God, for the many most glorious interpositions of his Providence manifested in a great and signal manner in behalf of these United States, during their conflict with one of the first powers of Europe: For rescuing them in the Day of Distress from tyranny and oppression, and supporting them with the aid of great and powerful allies: For conducting them gloriously and triumphantly through a just and necessary War, and putting an end to the calamities thereof by the restoration of Peace, after humbling the pride of our enemies and compelling them to acknowledge the Sovereignty and Independence of the American Empire, and relinquish all right and claim to the same: For raising up a distressed and Injured People to rank among independent nations and sovereign Powers of the world. And for all other divine favors bestowed on the Inhabitants of the United States and this in particular.

In conformity to the pious intentions of the Legislature I have thought proper to issue this my Proclamation directing that the said 4th Day of July next be observed as above, hereby strictly commanding and enjoining all the Good Citizens of this State to set apart the said Day from bodily labour, and employ the same in devout and religious exercises. And I do require all Ministers of the Gospel of every Denomination to convene their congregations at the same time, and deliver to them Discourses suitable to the important occasion recommending in general the practice of Virtue and true Religion as the great foundation of private blessing as well as National happiness and prosperity.

Given under my hand and the great Seal of the State at Danbury the 18th day of June in the year 1783 and seventh year of the Independence of the said State.

ALEX. MARTIN,
God save the State.

By his Excellency's Command.
P. Henderson Pro Sec.

Although there is a manuscript copy of the 18 June proclamation in the Salem archives, there is no indication of when it was received by the Moravians, nor was there any discussion of the coming holiday until a meeting of the Elders on 30 June 1783. Since the Salem Diary mentions that, on that day, "Governor Martin came here on his way to Salisbury and attended the *Singstunde*,"[4] it is likely that he brought the proclamation with him and presented it to the Elders on 30 June 1783.

As the first order of business at their 30 June meeting, the Elders began to make plans for the coming event:

[Monday, 30 June 1783] 1. Since the government has proclaimed 4 July as the Thanksgiving Festival of Peace, all congregations will be informed of this and everyone shall refrain from work on that day. Br. Marshall has prepared a circular to the country congregations to this effect.

For the celebration there will be a public Preaching Service where the Te Deum will be sung, and a Lovefeast for adults and children will be arranged, to which all visitors will be welcome.

Should the Governor wish to attend the Festival here, a formal table will be set for him in the tavern.[5]

When the Elders met again two days later, plans for the celebration were virtually complete. While the plans for the Peace Festival were less elaborate and prolonged than those made for the Assembly meetings held in the previous two years, the musical parts of the celebration are covered in much greater detail in the minutes of the meeting written by Friedrich Peter:

[Midweek (Wednesday), 2 July 1783] 2. At 10 o'clock, the Preaching Service will begin with the Te Deum, sung to trombone accompaniment. The text of the sermon will be the 46th Psalm, from which was drawn the Losung for 20 January, the day the Peace Preliminaries were signed. At the Lovefeast at 2 o'clock, a musical psalm of thanksgiving will be sung, and in the evening, after the hymn of praise: Praise be to Thee, that dwells above the Cherubim, is sung in the *Gemeinsaal*, there will be a procession with music and song through the town which will be illuminated, and at its termination in front of the *Gemeinhaus*, the Congregation will receive the Lord's Blessing.[6]

There is but one musical item used in the Fourth of July celebration—the anthem "Glory to God in the Highest," which closed the morning service[7]—that is not mentioned in the Elders Conference minutes.

While the impending festival required much attention from the Elders during this week, there was also another matter that was of grave concern to the town officials at this time. For several months, there had been growing unrest and dissension among the citizens of Salem who had been exposed to the freer way of life practiced by the many visitors and military men who had passed through Salem during the war years. Bickering over prices and defiance of the town's regulations reached such alarming proportions during the early summer of 1783 that the various governing boards felt compelled to take steps to forestall a complete breakdown of order.[8] Members of the *Aufseher Collegium* were informed on 10 June that "Brethren and Sisters are availing themselves of the advice and help of conjurers and wise women. It will be necessary to discuss this in Congregation Council, for there are such people ['Satan's assistants'] living not far from us."[9]

Meeting on 14 June 1783, the Elders decided that the conduct of the communicants warranted the withholding of Holy Communion,[10] and, in enumerating the reasons for this action, they cited opposition to congregation regulations, absence from services for the purpose of gathering socially in private homes, and the unauthorized meeting of unmarried members of the opposite sex in some of the family dwellings, which gave rise to gossip among the townspeople.[11]

On 19 June the Congregation Council discussed the situation at length:

For some time it has been evident that slander and backbiting have been prevalent in this town, and that almost no rule or arrangement can be made in the congregation without arousing opposition or rebellion. If the spirit of variance cannot be broken this time, it is sure to manifest itself at the next opportunity.

This condition has affected the services of the congregation, and few of the members from the upper town attend the *Singstunde*, and but few come to the Saturday prayer meeting. There is much opposition to the musical liturgy on Friday, and it appears that it is regarded as a burden, as it interferes with the private gatherings which have been taking place during the *Singstunde*. As innocent as may have been the beginning in one or another case, it is against all congregation rules, and contrary to the warnings of Synod, when such gatherings prevent members from attending the *Singstunden*. The same applies to the custom of sitting in front of the houses in summer, talking with the neighbors, for a member who is not going to service ought to be polite enough to go home when the bell rings, so as not to prevent others from going. These illegitimate gatherings lead to a kind of *independence* of rules and regulations, the actions of the ministers of the congregation are criticised, faults in them and in other members are pointed out, amplified, and often things that have no existence are told.[12]

To remedy the distressing situation, the Elders prescribed, among other things, the public recognition of "boys and girls who behave well,"[13] and the singing of hymn verses by the nightwatchman as he made his nightly rounds.[14]

At their meeting on 2 July, after learning the details of the Peace Celebration scheduled for the Fourth of July, the Elders were reminded that "Communion time is drawing near again. Communicants are asked to confer next Monday and Tuesday with the leaders of their Choirs so that we may ask the Saviour about the next Communion with more confidence."[15] During those conferences, held on 7 and 8 July after the Peace Festival, the communicants were found to be in "such a good frame of mind, having put away all misunderstanding among themselves, and so eager for the enjoyment of the Lord's Supper that we had no misgivings in announcing Communion."[16]

The changed attitude of the citizens resulted, at least in part, from the heartwarming effects of the Fourth of July festival. The sermon given on that morning had drawn a parallel between peace in the land and peace in the heart,[17] and "hearts were filled with the gentle Godly peace which prevailed the entire day and was felt in a particularly compelling manner during the procession."[18]

In writing the Wachovia Memorabilia for the year 1783, Friedrich Peter singled out both events for special comment:

What shall the congregation of Salem say about the Saviour? Truly He has loved us as children; that is proven by His fatherly dealings with us. When the spirit of extravagance and independence turned us from His way,

when we forgot His command to love Him and each other, He disciplined us for the restoration of our peace. Oh, how our mouths were filled with praise and thanksgiving when as forgiven sinners we might again partake of the Supper of the Lord. . . .

We bring to Him the heartfelt thanks which are due, in that He has given to us and to all congregations in America, yea to the whole land, the gift of honorable peace, for which we have sighed during eight years of the stress and alarm of war. . . . By order of the government of this State we celebrated a day of thanksgiving on July 4th, for the re-establishment of peace, and with all our hearts we rejoiced before the Lord our God with instrumental music and songs of joy. We still hold in thankful remembrance the blessed sabbatic peace of the entire day, and especially the evening procession.[19]

Any attempt to recreate that Day of Solemn Thanksgiving in Salem must rest on the initial research conducted by Adelaide L. Fries during the early part of this century.[20] Then archivist of the Moravian Church, Southern Province, Miss Fries had access to all the extant documents of the early Moravians in Wachovia and it was she who first came across the references to the Peace Celebration held on the Fourth of July, 1783, in Salem. In a short article describing the day, written in 1913 and published two years later,[21] Miss Fries gave a colorful, imaginative description of the afternoon Lovefeast and included her translations of a few parts[22] of the *Freudenpsalm* text that she had unearthed among the papers preserved in the Salem archives. However, since the music manuscripts dating from the late eighteenth century had not been assembled and organized, she made no attempt to identify the musical settings of the *Freudenpsalm* text; her description of the *Saal* in which the Lovefeast was held was also, by necessity, incomplete since the *Gemeinhaus* was no longer standing in 1913 and research on the design of the structure had not yet begun. While Miss Fries's article has provided footnotes for a number of articles and dissertations over the years, it did not generate further research into the subject until the current project began in 1966. During the fifty years that had elapsed, a considerable amount of work had been accomplished in the Moravian Archives: documents had been found and filed in retrievable order; music manuscripts had been assigned, at least tentatively, to their proper collections and their catalogs had been located; a general understanding of the role of music in the lives of the Moravians had been attained; and an imposing body of research materials had been amassed in connection with restoration projects in Old Salem. It was the proper time to reexamine the Day of Solemn Thanksgiving.[23]

The scene of the celebration was laid in the *Saal* of the *Gemeinhaus*, the dedication of which had been the first gala event held in Salem.[24] A large building situated at the northeast corner of the village square, the *Gemeinhaus*[25] (Plate 2) served in the early years of Salem as a lodging for the ministers and other church officials and as a temporary dwelling for the Single Sisters. The *Saal* (Figure C) was located on the second floor, in the center of the building between the two staircases. The south stairway connected the *Saal* with the section of the *Gemeinhaus* assigned to the Single Sisters, and, therefore, it was used only by the women of the congregation; men entered the *Gemeinhaus* through the north door and used the north staircase to reach the *Saal*. Thirty feet wide and thirty-six feet deep,[26] the *Saal* was flanked on the north by a conference room (15' × 25'), used by the Dieners[27] to prepare Lovefeast refreshments, and on the south by a smaller *Saal* (also 15' × 25') for the use of the Single Sisters' Choir meetings; on special occasions, the "Little *Saal*" was opened to accommodate the overflow crowds attending services held in the larger *Saal*.[28]

In the *Saal*, the minister's table, covered in black leather with a green skirt,[29] was placed at the center of the west wall facing the backless wooden benches on which the congregation was seated.[30] The sixteen benches[31] were arranged with a middle aisle[32] to accommodate the central supporting pillar, to separate the boys and men (seated on the north) from the girls and women (seated on the south), and to facilitate the serving of refreshments during Love-feasts; extra benches were placed around the walls of the *Saal*.[33] The eight windows (four in the east wall and four in the west) were hung with striped draperies that had replaced in 1781 the blue drapes that were part of the *Saal*'s original furnishings.[34]

The musicians occupied benches along the east wall, near the organ;[35] in 1783, those benches stood at floor level,[36] surrounding the organ. Since the music used on the Fourth of July required two choruses, often performing antiphonally, it can be assumed that the two groups were separated and placed on either side of the organ case. A logical seating arrangement for the orchestra would place instrumentalists near the singers whom they would accompany. For the Fourth of July music, this would entail the placing of the strings between the two choruses since they accompanied both groups; the wind instruments, i.e., flutes and horns, which played only when the first chorus sang, would be situated near that group; the brass choir, which led the congregational singing, might have occupied the benches normally reserved for the musicians at the rear wall on either side of the organ, or the players might have been arranged along the north and south walls to support the antiphonal singing between the men and the women of the congregation (Figure C).

The three events comprising the Fourth of July observance in Salem followed to the letter the dictates of the governor's proclamation; the "Day of Solemn Thanksgiving to Almighty God" consisted of appropriate "devout and religious exercises." Such exercises, of course, were not new to the Moravians, and, in fact, the three services lay within the normal framework of their devotional meetings with some modification and expansion to reflect the festal nature of the day. The morning service followed the order of the Preaching Service, shifted to Friday from its usual scheduling on Sunday; the evening *Sing-stunde* was more elaborate than usual to accommodate the outdoor procession that culminated the day's activities; the afternoon meeting was a typical Lovefeast, with food prepared in the conference room adjacent to the *Saal* and served during the singing of the *Freudenpsalm*.

While the Lovefeast held on the Fourth of July followed its usual pattern, the specific refreshments served on that day cannot be determined exactly, for the availability and cost of provisions influenced the choice of foods served at such functions. It is certain that each participant received a roll or sweet cake; the accompanying beverage may have been highly

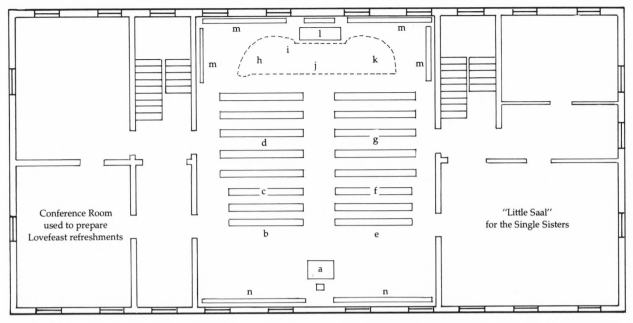

NORTH ◄────► SOUTH

F I G U R E C. *The* Saal *of the Salem Gemeinhaus.*
Drawing by Philip Martin.

sweetened coffee or tea, or *Buschwein.* The Lovefeast
Account[37] for 1783 lists purchases of coffee, tea,
sugar, milk, and *Buschwein,* but neither the dates of
the several Lovefeasts held during the year nor the
provisions used on each occasion are noted. Since the
Congregation Account for 1783[38] contains no
mention of special expenses incurred during the
Peace Festival, it is unlikely that more elaborate
refreshments were served during the Lovefeast, for
extra funds would have been drawn from one of the
two accounts.

The term *Buschwein* is not explained in the Moravian
records, but the minutes of a meeting of the *Helfer
Conferenz* held on 13 May 1776 may provide a clue to
its identity. During the meeting, it was noted that
"tea, coffee, and sugar are very expensive for use in
Lovefeasts. We discussed the possibility of using
wine, made from wild grapes mixed with *Marticelum,*
and decided to try it. We might use cider or currant
wine or blackberry wine."[39] The various kinds of
wine enumerated here may be the *Buschwein*
frequently mentioned in the records.[40]

In meetings held in May 1781, members of the Elders
Conference[41] and the *Aufseher Collegium*[42] discussed
the financial arrangements that should regulate
Lovefeasts, and from their deliberations comes a
great deal of information concerning the number of

people who normally attended Lovefeasts in Salem,
the amount and cost of food consumed, the recipes
for Lovefeast tea and coffee, and the price charged to
each person participating in the Lovefeast:[43]

For Ordinary (Communicants) Lovefeast,
  100 persons attending:

¼ lb. tea	-/6/-
3 lb. sugar	-/14/-
100 rolls	-/16/8
Milk and other things	-/2/-
Total expenses	£1/18/8

For Great (Congregation) Lovefeast,
  150 persons attending:

4 lb. coffee	-/16/-
6 lb. sugar	-/28/-
150 cakes	-/37/6
Milk and other things	-/3/-
Total expenses	£4/4/6

Price per person:

for Ordinary Lovefeasts	6 pence
for Great Lovefeasts	8 pence

The Lovefeast held during the 1783 Peace Festival
would certainly fall into the classification of "Great
Lovefeast" since it was open to visitors as well as all
adults and children of the congregation, which

consisted of approximately 180 persons in 1783.[44] The *Saal* would have been filled to its capacity at the Lovefeast, as well as at the other services conducted on that day. One of the principal features of every meeting would be music, for, according to Moravian custom, to hear the choir of musicians perform the concerted anthems and to join in singing hymns of praise was to properly observe such an important day.

As musical director, Friedrich Peter assumed the responsibility for preparing the music for the Peace Festival. Since he also acted as secretary to the Elders Conference, he was present during the meeting on 30 June when the first tentative plans were made to hold two services to mark the occasion.[45] At that meeting, only one musical composition was selected, the Te Deum, which would be sung at the morning Preaching Service; though not mentioned in the minutes of the 30 June meeting, tradition demanded that a fairly elaborate musical program be presented during the Lovefeast, which was scheduled for the afternoon. With but four days in which to select and rehearse music for the Fourth of July, Peter could not hope to compose new music especially for the occasion. He must use whatever he could find in the music library that would be appropriate to a celebration of peace, and there had been little peace since the library was begun. From existing records, the process by which Peter arranged the Fourth of July schedule of events and selected proper music for each event can be reconstructed step by step.

A precedent for the Salem Peace Festival had been established in the German Moravian communities where similar observances were held at the close of the Seven Years' War in 1763. Peter had been a seventeen-year-old student in the Moravian schools in Germany at the time, and, twenty years later, he would remember those festivals as he began to plan the Salem events. Furthermore, housed in his own lodgings in Salem, among the archival papers in his custody as archivist of the town, were copies of the official accounts of the 1763 German celebrations and those accounts contained detailed descriptions of the several services held in the various Moravian settlements with specific references to the music used in each service.[46]

The progress report Peter submitted to the Elders on 2 July contains evidence that, during the forty-eight hours that had elapsed since the first discussion of the proposed celebration, he had studied some of the accounts of the 1763 peace festivals. In Gnadenberg,[47] an evening service featured the Te Deum sung to trombone accompaniment[48] and, as night fell, lights were placed in the windows of all the houses in the village as a symbol of the end of the darkness of war. The Moravian Seminary in Barby,[49] where Peter was a student, was also illuminated, with appropriate texts silhouetted against the light: in the upper windows appeared the word *Friede* (Peace) and in the center of the building was placed the sentence "Mitten wir im Kriege hat Er uns erhalten" ("In the midst of the war He has sustained us"), a quotation from the liturgy that Christian Gregor had set to music in 1759, at the height of the Seven Years' War. That afternoon in Barby, the same quotation had been used to decorate the table at the Lovefeast during which Gregor's setting of that liturgy, *Gelobt seyst du, der du sizest über Cherubim*, was sung.[50]

Drawing several ideas from the Barby and Gnadenberg celebrations, Peter began to fill in the details of the Salem celebration. At the Elders meeting on 2 July[51] it was agreed that the Te Deum, which had already been selected to open the morning service, would be accompanied by the trombones.[52] The Elders also approved the addition of a third service—an evening gathering that would take the form of a modified *Singstunde*. Beginning in the *Saal* with a performance of Gregor's *Gelobt seyst du, der du sizest über Cherubim*, the meeting would move outdoors and continue with a procession through the illuminated town while the chorales were played and sung. It was also announced at the 2 July meeting that a "musikalischer *Dankpsalm*" would be sung during the afternoon Lovefeast, but, since no further details are given in the minutes of that meeting, it can be assumed that the *Dankpsalm*, the most elaborate of the musical offerings for the day, was not complete at that time: for Friedrich Peter, there was still much work to be done in the next forty-eight hours before the Lovefeast music would be ready for performance.

The manner in which the various movements of the Salem Lovefeast music were selected and arranged in order can be deduced by examining and comparing the extant copies of the Lovefeast Psalm text[53] with texts supplied in the accounts of the 1763 German peace festivals, for in planning the Salem Lovefeast music Peter again turned to those accounts for ideas. Of particular help to Peter were the accounts of the celebrations held in Herrnhut[54] and in Gnadenfrey,[55] since both accounts contain the full texts for the Psalms performed in those communities during the festivals.[56] Though Peter may have had copies of the musical settings of the two 1763 Psalms in his personal library, the Salem collection of musical parts did not contain complete musical settings of either Psalm, so he could not merely schedule a performance of one or the other of the earlier Psalms; he must use the musical resources available in Salem. The 1763 Psalms were, themselves, compilations of various compositions drawn from several different sources; it was common practice for Moravian musicians to adapt preexistent music of all kinds to suit the musical needs of the moment.[57] Therefore, in compiling the Fourth of July Psalm from the miscellaneous materials at hand, Peter was merely following the accepted procedure.

From the Gnadenfrey Psalm, Peter chose two recitatives, "Der Herr ist der rechte Kriegsmann" and "Er schliesst an allen Orten die Jammer-Pforten," and a duet, "Das Land wird ruhig." In looking over the anthem texts given in the 1763 Psalms, Peter had to take into account the availability of musical settings for those texts. If the Salem library did not have performers' parts for a suitable setting of a text, there was no point in considering that text, and, even if there were parts, the composition must be one that the Salem musicians could perform with little or no rehearsal. With these factors in mind, Peter chose from the Gnadenfrey Psalm one anthem text, "Jauchzet dem Herrn," since the Salem library had parts for a setting of a similar text that, even in its altered version, would be a suitable anthem for a celebration of peace. In all, the Gnadenfrey Psalm provided suitable texts for four compositions to be included in the Salem Lovefeast Psalm.

From the Danck- und Freudenpsalm text given in the account of the Herrnhut peace festival, Peter selected for the Salem Lovefeast music an appropriate hymn

text, "Du gibst Fried in unserm Lande," which he modified to read "Gott gib Fried in diesem Lande," and two anthem texts, "Das ist ein Tag" and "Dass in unserm Lande" that concluded with a hymn quotation sung as a response by the congregation. To the musical portion of the morning service reported on 2 July,[58] Peter now added an anthem, *Ehre sey Gott in der Höhe*, from the Herrnhut Psalm. Gregor's setting of that text was a particular favorite in the Salem community; the fifth composition to be placed in the library, it had seen constant use over the years.

With the aid of the accounts of the 1763 peace festivals, Peter had worked out the complete musical programs for the morning Preaching Service and the evening *Singstunde*-Procession:

Morning (complete)
    Te Deum, with trombone accompaniment
    Anthem: *Ehre sey Gott in der Höhe*
Evening (complete)
    Liturgy: *Gelobt seyst du, der du sizest über Cherubim*
    Unspecified chorales for the procession

and the Psalm for the afternoon Lovefeast was beginning to take shape:

Afternoon (incomplete)*
  [II]   Anthem: "Das ist ein Tag"
  [III]   Anthem: "Jauchzet dem Herrn"
          (modified version in Salem)
  [V]   Recitative: "Der Herr ist der rechte
          Kriegsmann"
  [VII]   Duet: "Das Land wird ruhig"
  [IX]   Recitative: "Er schliesst an allen Orten"
  [XIV]   Chorale: "Gott gib Fried in diesem
          Lande" (modified version)
  [XV]   Anthem: "Dass in unserm Lande" with
          Chorale Response

To this list of compositions Peter added one more anthem, selecting from the folio of parts containing "Jauchzet dem Herrn" a composition of similar character, "Preise, Jerusalem, den Herrn"; the additional anthem placed after "Dass in unserm Lande" would provide a suitable ending to the portions of the Psalm assigned to the Choir of

*Bracketed roman numerals indicate the position of each composition within the completed Psalm.

Musicians, and, at the same time, would form with its neighbor a pair of closing anthems [XV + XVI] to balance the opening pair [II + III].

Having settled on the concerted music to be used in the Lovefeast Psalm, Peter needed only to select some chorales to complete the afternoon musical program. Following Moravian custom, new verses appropriate to the occasion would be sung to the familiar tunes. The identity of the author (or authors) of the ten new verses included in the Salem Lovefeast Psalm is not known, but Moravians were prolific versifiers and several authors, including Peter,[59] could have contributed original hymn verses for the celebration.

By the afternoon of the Fourth of July—four days after the celebration was first discussed in Salem—the Lovefeast Psalm was ready for performance. In addition to selecting and rehearsing the music, Peter had joined with other copyists in preparing enough handwritten copies of the Psalm text for distribution to the musicians and congregation, all of whom would need to follow the text during the Lovefeast service. The Psalm text followed by the participants in the Lovefeast, complete with indications of the group assigned to perform each segment of the Psalm, reads:[60]

Freudenpsalm
Der Gemeine in Salem
zum Friedens-Dankfeste.
d. 4. Juli 1783[61]

[I.]   *Chorus I.*
Es ist Friede! es ist Friede!
Freu dich, Volk des HErrn![62]

Chorus II.
Es ist Friede! es ist Friede!
Ey das hört man gern!

Gem.[63]   Friede! welch ein edles Wort!
Friede schall' nun immerfort!

Alle Brr.[64]
Friede, Friede!

Alle Schwn.[65]
Friede, Friede!

Alle.[66]   Friede kommt vom HErrn!

[II.]   *Chorus II.*
Das ist ein Tag, den der HErr gemacht hat; lasset uns freuen und fröhlich darinnen seyn.

[III.]   *Chorus I.*
Jauchzet dem HErrn alle Welt, singet, rühmet und lobet; jauchzet alle vor dem HErrn, dem Könige; alle

Seine Heerschaaren, frohlocket Seinem Namen; frohlocket, ihr starken Helden, die ihr Seinen Befehl ausrichtet; preiset und rühmet den HERRN, ja preiset den HERRN. Der Himmel freue sich und die Erde sey fröhlich; das Meer brause, und was darinnen ist; das Feld sey fröhlich und alles, was drauf ist, und lasset rühmen alle Bäume im Walde. Alles Land bete Ihn an, und lobsinge Seinem Namen; Er hat herrliche Thaten gethan; Er hat grosse Thaten gethan! Selah![67]

[IV.]   *Gem.*[68]
Freudenvoll lasst uns nun singen,
Und unserm Gott Dankopfer bringen
Für Seine grosse Wunderthat!

Schreckenvoll auf allen Seiten
Sah man die Kriegswut sich ausbreiten,
Die unser Land erschüttert hat.

Es ward fast nichts gehört,
Als Feind und Feur und Schwerdt,[69]
Noth und Jammer.
Wie oft rief ich ganz ängstiglich:
"Sieh drein, o Gott! erbarme Dich!"

[V.]   *Recitativ.*

Der HErr ist der rechte Kriegsmann, Jehovah ist Sein Name, der den Kriegen steuert in aller Welt, der Bogen, Schwerdt und Schild zerbricht, Spiesse zerschlägt, und Wagen mit Feuer verbrennet. Das Land ist allenthalben jämmerlich verwüstet, und die Häuser sind zerrissen. Weil nun die Elenden verstöret werden, und die Armen seufzen, will ich auf, spricht der HErr: Alle Krieger müssen die Hände lassen sinken. Denn ich will auf, spricht der HErr, sie müssen die Hände lassen sinken.[70]

[VI.]   *Gem.*

Du bist GOtt :/: Jesu, du Gekreuzigter!
Gottes Lamm, für uns geschlachtet,
Du bist aller Herren HErr!
Legst auch den, der Dich verachtet,
In den Staub troz aller Feinde Spott;
Du bist Gott :/:

Chorus I.
Jauchzet, unser Freund ist König!
Alles ist Ihm unterthänig;

Chorus II.
Alles legt sich Ihm zu Füssen;
Alles wird sich beugen müssen.

Gem.
Er allein soll es seyn, unser Gott und HErre;
Ihm gebührt die Ehre![71]

[VII.]   *Duetto.*

Das Land wird ruhig; denn der HErr schaft unsern Grenzen Friede.

[VIII.]   *Gem.*

Sing, o meine Seele! singe!
Sing dem Friedefürsten Dank!
Furchtbar war der Gang der Dinge,
Doch mein Glaube ward nicht krank!
Trübsal zeigte[72] sich in Menge,
Und es kam auch mancher Schlag,
Den man *schrecklich*[73] nennen mag.
Aber mitten im Gedränge
Sprach ich: ''Der mich trägt und hebt,
Jesus, mein Erlöser lebt.''

[IX.]   *Recitativ.*

Er schliesst an allen Orten die Jammerpforten; auch unser Land erholet sich, nachdem sichs satt geseufzet hat.

[X.]   *Arietta.*[74]
Chorus I.   Ach wie die Ruh so gütlich,
                So wohl so sanfte thut!

Chorus II.   Wie hat mans so gemütlich,
                Wenn man im Friede ruht!

Beyde Chöre.[75]   Da können die Erlösten
                    Sich mit den Worten trösten:
                    Wir, Deine Schäfelein,
                    Gehn friedsam aus und ein.

[XI.]   *Gem.*
Ehre sey GOtt in der Höhe,
Und Friede in der Fern und Nähe;
Denn unser Friedefürst ist da!
GOtt ist selbst in unsrer Mitten!
Gemeine freu dich deiner Hütten,
Der bey uns wohnt ist Jehovah!
Er hat von Stuhl und Stab
Besiz und lässt nicht ab[76]
Uns zu segnen.
Er schenkt voll ein,
Und Gross und Klein[77]
Kann Seines Schuzes sich erfreun.

[XII.]   *Solo.*[78]
HErr! lass die Unität,
Die diesen Segen
Uns von Dir hat erfleht,
Auf Deinen Wegen
Des Friedens in dem Land
Die Freude sehen,
Dass Deiner Hände Werk
Durch Deine Kraft und Stärk
Mag weiter gehen.

[XIII.]   *Beyde Chöre.*[79]
Gruss Deinen Segen reichlich aus,
So weit die Wolken gehen:
Lass Kirche, Regiment und Haus

In gutem Stande stehen!
Gib Frieden in der Christenheit,
Lass Gottesfurcht und Einigkeit
In allen Ländern grünen,
Und alle Welt Dir dienen.

[XIV.]   *Gem.*
   Gott gib Fried in diesem Lande; Glück und Heil
zu allem Stande!

[XV.]   *Chorus I.*
   Dass in unserm Lande Ehre wohne, dass Güte und
Treue einander begegnen, Gerechtigkeit und Friede
sich küssen, dass Treue auf der Erde wachse und
Gerechtigkeit vom Himmel schaue; dass unser Land
sein Gewächs gebe, und Er sättige alles, was da
lebet,[80] mit Wohlgefallen, und dass alles Ihn suchen
und finden möge, und Seine Gemeinen gehen und
sich bauen.

                    Gem.
   Das walt, der es heisst, der Vater, der Sohn und
der heilige Geist.

[XVI.]   *Chorus I.*
   Preise, Jerusalem, den HErrn; lobe Zion Deinen
GOtt; Jünglinge und Jungfrauen, Alte mit den

Jungen sollen loben den Namen des HErrn. Die
Gemeine der Heiligen soll Ihn loben. Sie sollen loben
Seinen Namen im Reigen; mit Pauken und Harfen
sollen sie Ihm spielen. Lobet Ihn in Seinen Thaten;
lobet Ihn in Seiner grossen Herrlichkeit; lobet Ihn
mit Posaunen und Psalter und Reigen; lobet Ihn mit
Saiten und Pfeiffen; lobet Ihn mit hellen Cymbeln,
lobet Ihn mit wohlklingenden Cymbeln. Alles, was
Othem hat, lobe den HErrn, Hallelujah!

[XVII.]   *Alle.*
   Hallelujah, ohn Aufhören!
   Aus allen Kräften lasst uns ehren
   Den Vater, Sohn und heilgen Geist!
   Solches Lob klingt hier schon lieblich;
   Wie aber wirds erst seyn, wie herrlich,
   Wenn man Ihn dort vollkommen preist!
   Dort, dort im Friedenssaal
   Beym grossen Abendmahl.
      Hallelujah!

Alle Brr.[81]   Heilig ist Gott!

Alle Schwn.[82]   Heilig ist Gott!

Alle.   Heilig, heilig, heilig ist GOtt!

When the Day of Solemn Thanksgiving was ended,
the people of Salem turned their attention to other
matters.[83] A few copies of the *Freudenpsalm* text were
saved to include in the official accounts of the
celebration and the musical parts used during the
observance were returned to the music library to be
used again for other occasions. No record was kept of
the concerted music and chorale tunes that had been
performed on the Fourth of July, 1783. Consequently,
the modern restoration of the musical events
surrounding the observance required a great deal of
preliminary detective work.

A search through the Salem music collections
confirmed the fact that there were no notations on
any manuscripts that clearly indicated their use on
the Fourth of July. The restoration, then, must rely on

clues provided in these sources: (1) minutes of the
Elders Conference meetings held on 30 June and
2 July 1783[84] when plans were drawn for the peace
celebration; (2) Friedrich Peter's description of the
observance as it appears in the Salem Diary and its
extracts;[85] and (3) the *Freudenpsalm* text (given above
in its entirety) which is filed with the diary. Those
clues must be tested against the musical resources[86]
known to be available in 1783: (1) the collection of
chorale tunes preserved in the partbooks (Plate 7)
used by the brass choir in Salem during the 1780s;[87]
and (2) for concerted music, the voluminous library
of musical parts in manuscript form. Unfortunately
for this project, the collection is now arranged in the
order established during its reorganization in 1808,
which destroyed the previous chronological arrange-

ment of the compositions within the library and, therefore, presented numerous obstacles in determining precisely the availability of particular compositions to Salem musicians in 1783.[88]

Locating the music performed at the morning and evening meetings on the Fourth of July was a relatively simple task. For the Te Deum, which opened the morning Preaching Service, a four-part harmonization is supplied in the extant partbooks used by the Salem brass choir; parts for the anthem *Ehre sey Gott in der Höhe* by Christian Gregor, which closed the morning service, were available to the choir of musicians in at least three different manuscripts in 1783, and portions of all these manuscripts survive. Gregor's original (1759) setting of *Gelobt seyst Du*, sung at the evening *Singstunde*-Procession, had been replaced by its 1791 revision in the Salem Collections, but a score of the earlier version is preserved in the Johannes Herbst Collection.

Identifying and locating all the music for the afternoon Lovefeast Psalm, however, presented many challenges that taxed both human and historical resources. The search began in January 1966 and ended successfully—and accidentally—in August 1968. The two and a half years devoted to the project were filled with equal parts of frustrating failures and exhilarating successes. What follows is a personal, chronological account of the long, almost obsessive search.

In January 1966 there was no real precedent for this kind of research project in Moravian music. Two years earlier, for the rededication of the restored Single Brothers' House in Salem, the Right Reverend Kenneth G. Hamilton and I had collaborated in an attempt to reconstruct the Psalm sung at the original dedication of the building in 1769. That Psalm, however, had consisted entirely of newly composed hymn texts set in Common Meter (8.6.8.6.) for which the Moravians had at least a dozen tunes that they could have used. Since there was no way to determine precisely which tunes the Brothers chose to sing in 1769, our "reconstruction" could be only an approximation of the original dedicatory Psalm. Knowing from this earlier experience that a positive

identification of all the Lovefeast music might be impossible, I approached the Fourth of July project with some trepidation. The only clues would be those found on the *Freudenpsalm* text.

When the project began, only one copy of the *Freudenpsalm* text had been found, i.e., the copy (SA) filed with the Salem Diary; the full text of that copy is transcribed on pages 24–26 of this volume. On examining that copy, it became clear that the *Freudenpsalm* text represented a much more ambitious musical program than the Brothers' House dedicatory Psalm had proven to be. There are passages in poetry alternating with prose sections, and various groups are cited as performers of the several segments of the Psalm. The prose sections are labeled *Chorus I, Chorus II, Duetto,* or *Recitativ,* indicating that only trained musicians had performed these sections. The segments of poetry, however, are assigned to several different groups, including *Gem.* (congregation), *Alle* (everyone), *Alle Brr.* (all men), *Alle Schwn.* (all women), *Chorus I, Chorus II,* and *Solo.* Since everyone attending the Lovefeast joined at one time or another in singing these parts of the *Freudenpsalm,* the poems must be hymns set to tunes that would be familiar to everyone. The scriptural source of the prose passages suggested that those assigned to the choruses are texts of concerted anthems that might be found among the hundreds of manuscripts filed in the Salem Collection. Aware of the fact that an identification of the specific chorale tunes used in the *Freudenpsalm* might be difficult, if not impossible, that part of the project was postponed until it could be determined whether or not the anthems could be found.

In 1966 a massive cataloging project was under way in which a modern catalog of one collection of music manuscripts was virtually completed. That collection, the Johannes Herbst Collection of scores, would be of invaluable assistance in the current study, but it could be used only for reference purposes, since it was not a part of the Salem library in 1783. If there were to be any claim of authenticity for the Fourth of July music, the anthems must be found among the manuscripts used by Salem musicians in 1783, that is, the Salem Collection of musical parts. Cataloging this collection had not yet begun, but the manuscripts were filed in at least a semblance of order according to catalogs of the collection prepared in 1808, and materials could be located with some difficulty. There was the strong possibility that the collection would contain several settings of the texts used in the *Freudenpsalm*, and some means must be found to decide which setting was actually sung on the Fourth of July, 1783. Friedrich Peter had borrowed three of the anthem texts from the *Danck-Psalms* performed in Herrnhut and Gnadenfrey, Germany, during the 1763 peace festivals; if he also borrowed the music and that music could be found in Salem, the search for anthems would be short. Only the Herrnhut music was found, and that is in the Johannes Herbst Collection of scores—not a part of the Salem Collection, but it provided a starting point for the project.

Two of the anthem texts, "Das ist ein Tag" [II] and "Dass in unserm Lande" [XV], are part of the 1763 Herrnhut *Danck-Psalm* so these anthems were the first to be considered. In checking through all the available catalogs of Moravian music collections in America (Herbst, Salem, Bethlehem, Lititz, and Nazareth), there appeared to be only one setting of "Dass in unserm Lande" in the Moravian repertoire and that must have been the setting used at the Herrnhut peace festival. Parts for this composition were found in the Salem Collection filed in Folio 154, a number that seemed to be too high in a collection that consisted of only 200 folios in 1808, twenty-five years after the *Freudenpsalm* was performed; on the other hand, the composition must have been used in 1783 since there is no other setting of the text. A manuscript's present folio number in the Salem Collection and its connection, if any, with the date that the manuscript entered the collection presented a problem that must be resolved before the search for the *Freudenpsalm* anthems could continue.

Some help toward a solution to the problem was found in a mysterious little document that, in 1966, had not been fully identified or studied.[89] Entitled *Anmerckungen beym durchsehen der Musicalien der Gemeine in Salem. Mart. 1808* (Observations in connection with the review of the congregation music in Salem. March, 1808), the document appeared to be an inventory of the 200 folios then comprising the Salem Collection. In the list of folios, few compositions are identified by title, but composers' names frequently appear in the left margin beside a folio number. Assuming that the folio numbers represent, at least roughly, the order in which compositions were added to the collection, some hint of the size of the library in the 1780s might be found by examining the names of composers given in the inventory, looking in particular for the name of Friedrich Peter, musical director in Salem during that time. While attempting to build the musical program during his first months in Salem, Peter might have added many of his compositions to the collection and, after this initial spurt, his contributions to the repertoire might have subsided gradually; he would send few, if any, compositions to Salem after his departure in 1790. Looking down the list of folio numbers in the *Anmerckungen*, Friedrich Peter's name is first seen beside Number 35 and then it is found with increasing frequency, appearing thirty-three times in the next fifty numbers. After Number 85, Peter's name appears less and less until it disappears altogether in the last 50 folios. Although inexact and not conclusive, this information gained by scanning the inventory raised the possibility that in 1780, when Peter arrived in Salem, the music library contained about 30 folios of parts and that during his ten years as musical director, he increased the size of the collection to approximately 150 folios. By 1783, the collection could have contained around 100 folios. If these figures are taken into account, and the collection did not contain 154 folios until after 1790, then Folio 154 containing "Dass in unserm Lande" [XV] was not in existence in 1783.

Fortunately, the *Anmerckungen* contributed more encouraging information concerning the numbering system used before the 1808 reorganization of the collection; a comparison of the folio number assigned in the *Anmerckungen* to a composition that could be identified by title and composer with the number now used for the same composition revealed the fact that a large proportion of the 200 folios were renumbered in the course of the 1808 reorganization. Therefore, the present numbers assigned to compositions are of importance only in locating a manuscript; it is the original ("old") number, which survives on many manuscripts, that helps to determine whether or not a manuscript might have been available in 1783. During this project, an upper limit of 100 was tentatively adopted as the cutoff point for "old" numbers which might have been available in 1783. The original number for "Dass in unserm Lande" [XV] was found to be Number 69, well within the self-imposed limits, and the first of the four *Freudenpsalm* anthems had been found.

The search for the second anthem text included in the Herrnhut *Danck-Psalm* also began with the score of the Herrnhut music preserved in the Herbst Collection. There it was discovered that the text "Das ist ein Tag" [II] is part of a large, bipartite anthem beginning "Gelobet sey der Herr! denn Er hat erhöret die Stimme unsers Flehens"; the second part of the anthem begins with "Das ist ein Tag" but continues with additional text that Peter did not include in his *Freudenpsalm*. Peter must have borrowed merely the text segment, intending to use a different musical setting, for the Salem Collection does not have parts for the Herrnhut version of the text. The 1808 Salem catalog does contain entries for two other settings of the text; one setting, listed as *"Dis* ist ein Tag," could not have been used in the *Freudenpsalm* if its composer, Weber, is the Gottfried Weber (1779–1839) whose works appear late in the Herbst Collection, for he would have been but four years old in July 1783. The other setting of the text preserved in the Salem Collection is found within Christian Gregor's anthem beginning "Zion hörts," composed in 1761. It seemed unlikely that Friedrich Peter would include a fragment of an anthem in the *Freudenpsalm*, but when the manuscript was located and the various musical parts were examined it became obvious that Peter did exactly that. The *Freudenpsalm* text is situated in the second and third parts of the anthem, which are connected to the first section without pause, so that separation of those sections is difficult and the results are awkward; furthermore, at the beginning of the second section, the various vocal parts present a confusing mixture of pronouns,[90] none of which agree with the *Freudenpsalm* version beginning *"Das ist ein* Tag." It was tempting to rule out this setting purely on textual and structural grounds, but the instrumental parts had not yet been studied. Among them is a ragged Organo part that has managed to

survive even though a newer organ part is included in the folio; on the old part is its original folio number, 53, and the date 1780 (Plate 4). There could be no doubt now that the manuscript was available in 1783. The last piece of evidence needed to identify this composition as part of the *Freudenpsalm* music was found in the old Organo part and the string parts: at the beginning of the second section of the anthem, a flag is drawn in red ink with a notation in what appears to be Friedrich Peter's handwriting: "Das ist ein tag"—the precise wording found in the *Freudenpsalm* text. The red flag had been used as a cue marking for the musicians who performed the *Freudenpsalm* (Plates 5 and 6).

The Salem catalogs list three entries under "Preise, Jerusalem, den HErrn" [XVI], but, when examining the vocal parts of each composition, it was discovered that two of the anthems contain only the first portion of the *Freudenpsalm* text while the third anthem sets the entire text. The latter is obviously the correct setting; its original folio number, 101, is but one notch above the cutoff point tentatively set at the beginning of the search. As a final step in its identification, the composition was checked with the Herbst Collection where the name of Johann Christian Geisler[91] is given as its composer and 1768 as the date of its composition; in the intervening fifteen years, the parts for the anthem could easily have found their way into the Salem Collection.

In the same Folio 101, and usually on the same page of manuscript, are the parts for another anthem by Geisler, setting a text that begins "Jauchzet dem HErrn," the same beginning used in the *Freudenpsalm* anthem text [III] that remained to be discovered. What appeared to be a lucky shortcut to identifying the last anthem was in actuality the beginning of a long period of indecision for, in reading through the text on the vocal parts, numerous differences and omissions from the corresponding *Freudenpsalm* text were noticed. The texts are similar but not identical and, having relied so heavily on textual factors in establishing the identity of the settings for "Preise, Jerusalem, den HErrn" and "Das ist ein Tag," the differences in this setting of "Jauchzet dem HErrn" could not be ignored. On the other hand, the Salem catalogs list no other settings under "Jauchzet dem

HErrn'' and the presence of both anthems in one manuscript would simplify the logistics of performing the *Freudenpsalm*, for there would be one less part for each performer to shuffle during the Lovefeast. With misgivings that would persist for two years, the decision was made to include this setting as part of the *Freudenpsalm* on a tentative basis, continuing to look for alternative settings or verification of this setting.

A thorough search through the Salem catalogs and manuscript collections for settings of the remaining prose passages—the two recitatives and the duet— also proved discouraging; there was no trace of them. Perhaps they had belonged to Friedrich Peter and he had taken them with him when he left Salem, or perhaps the soloists who performed them at the Fourth of July Lovefeast had carried them off. No matter what the reason for their absence, the recitatives and the duet could not be found in Salem. It was time to suspend work on the prose sections and turn to the ten hymn texts included in the *Freudenpsalm*; with luck, the Gnadenfrey *Danck-Psalm* music would appear one day and the missing settings for the prose sections of the *Freudenpsalm* would be found.

To locate the tunes accompanying the various hymns in the *Freudenpsalm*, the meter and rhyme scheme of each poem must be checked against the tunes known to have been used in Salem during the 1780s. The only definitive tune source dating from that period is the set of partbooks belonging to the *Posaunenchor*, since the organists' choralebook has disappeared; however, the choralebook compiled by Christian Gregor and published in 1784 proved to be a valuable reference tool. Recalling the uniformity of texts that had appeared in the dedicatory Psalm for the Single Brothers' House, the *Freudenpsalm* hymns were approached with some apprehension, but a quick check of the texts allayed all fears of such uniformity. The *Freudenpsalm* poets had employed a variety of poetic structures and none could be categorized as Common Meter or Short Meter. With few problems, the specific tune for each poem was determined and located among the chorales known to have been in use in Salem at the time of the Peace Celebration; with but one exception, each tune chosen could be

verified as the only available tune that would fit a given text. The tune numbers given below are the traditional numbers found in all Moravian chorale-books since 1755.

[I] ''Es ist Friede! es ist Friede!''

$$(8.5\,|\,8.5\,|\,7.7\,|\,8.5)$$
$$\text{or} \qquad = \text{Tune } 56$$
$$(4+4.5\,|\,4+4.5\,|\,7.7\,|\,4+4.5)$$

The *Freudenpsalm* poet followed the repetition scheme found in the hymn text usually associated with this tune, e.g., ''Ich wills wagen, ich wills wagen.''

[IV] ''Freudenvoll
    lasst uns nun singen''

[XI] ''Ehre sey Gott in
    der Höhe''

[XVII] ''Hallelujah
    ohn Aufhören''

$$(8.9.8\,|\,8.9.8\,|\,6.6.4\,|\,8.8)$$
$$\text{or} \qquad = \text{Tune } 230$$
$$(8.9.8\,|\,8.9.8\,|\,6.6.4\,|\,4+4.8)$$

After this tune was selected, another copy of the *Freudenpsalm* text (MMF) was found on which the notation ''Mel. Wachet auf'' appears (Plate 3), verifying the accuracy of the identification.

[VI] ''Du bist Gott ./. Jesu, du Gekreuzigter''

$$= \text{Tune } 119$$

To find a suitable setting for this text was the most difficult task in the tune-identification phase of the project. The first six lines, assigned to the congregation, follow the metrical scheme $3+3.7\,|\,8.7\,|\,8.9\,|\,3+3$ or $6.7\,|\,8.7\,|\,8.9\,|\,6$, for which Tune 119 is designed. The *Freudenpsalm* poem also follows the repetition pattern found in the text usually sung to this tune, e.g., ''Fahre fort, fahre fort''; line six is a restatement of the initial text and melody, rounding off the stanza. The next four lines (7 through 10), divided between Chorus I and Chorus II, are set in $8.8\,|\,8.8$, which implies trochaic Long Meter (Tune 23). The penultimate line, ''Er allein soll es seyn, unser Gott und HErre,'' sung by the congregation, reverts to the first metrical scheme with a modification: 3+3.7 becomes 3+3.6; despite its modification, line 11 seems to require the use of the opening section of Tune 119. The lacking syllable can be accommodated by slurring the appropriate notes within the phrase, in the manner suggested by Christian Gregor in the preface to his *Choralbuch* (1784). In the same preface, Gregor provides the solution to a problem arising with the last text line, "Ihm gebührt die Ehre," which has the same syllabification (6) as its partner in rhyme, "unser Gott und HErre," the last phrase of line 11. Gregor recommends that, in singing chorales, repetition for emphasis should be encouraged, and his advice has been heeded here in setting the last line of this text to the same musical phrase as its rhyming partner. Having settled on the congregation's sections of this text, the tune for the chorus sections must now be determined. The possibility of inserting Tune 23 for the chorus sections (lines 7 through 10 = 8.8 | 8.8, L. M.) was explored and found to be unsuitable, if for no other reason than the obvious fact that the keys of the two chorales (Tune 119 = D major, Tune 23 = F major) are incompatible. The chorus sections must be included within Tune 119 in some acceptable fashion. Christian Gregor's choralebook preface again came to the rescue. Gregor's suggestion that notes be slurred to accommodate a shortened text line is balanced by his opposite suggestion that long notes be divided into shorter, repeated notes to fit a lengthened text line. By utilizing both suggestions, the chorus sections can be brought into Tune 119 in a manner that underscores the related thoughts contained in the text segments set to the same musical phrases, inserts a bit of musical description in lines 4, 5, 9, and 10 (see score, p. 95), and makes sense musically. The manipulation of Tune 119, following Gregor's advice, results in a textual and musical unity:

Text: 3+3.7 | 8.7 | 8.9 | 3+3 || 8.8$^{(7)}$ | 8.8$^{(9)}$ || 3+3.6$^{(7)}$+6$^{(7)}$
Music: a b | c | d | a || c d || a b b
    Congregation   Chorus   Congregation

It should be noted that, in keeping with other suggestions offered by Gregor, Friedrich Peter assigned to the trained musicians those parts of the text that stray from the normal course of the chorale tune.

[VIII] "Sing, o meine Seele! singe"
        (8.7 | 8.7 | 8.7.7 | 8.7.7) = Tune 214A

Gregor's *Choralbuch* contains two tunes that fit the meter of this text; it is not known whether the Salem organbook also was supplied with two tunes. The choice of Tune 214A over 214B entailed both a practical and a musical decision. From the practical standpoint, since Tune 214B is not included among the chorales found in the Salem partbooks, and its presence in the missing organbook cannot be established, its use in Salem during the 1780s cannot be documented and, therefore, Tune 214B should not be selected for the *Freudenpsalm* text. From a musical standpoint, Tune 214B, consisting of two repeated sections, cannot follow the sense of the *Freudenpsalm* poem as closely as does 214A with its through-composed second section that begins at a low pitch level and climbs to a melodic peak as the text states optimistically: "Jesus, my Redeemer lives." The latter tune, Tune 214A, was selected to accompany this portion of the *Freudenpsalm* (pp. 101–3 of the edition); the text set to Tune 214B is given here so that the two possible versions can be compared; Tune 214B is transcribed from the 1784 *Choralbuch* compiled by Christian Gregor (see score on the following page).

[X] *Arietta*: "Ach wie die Ruh so gütlich"
                    = Tune 151A

This text presented two related problems, i.e., the choice of tune and the manner in which the tune was performed on the Fourth of July, 1783. Neither the Salem partbooks nor Gregor's *Choralbuch* contain tunes that fit the meter (7.6 | 7.6 | 7.7 | 6.6)[92] but, by applying Gregor's hints on slurring some notes and dividing others, those tunes classed as 151 (7.6 | 7.6 | 7.6 | 7.6) can be modified to fit the poem without sacrificing the integrity of the melodies or the text. Friedrich Peter's use of the heading *Arietta* implies that he intended this hymn to receive treatment other than the unison singing of the tune with an instrumental harmonization employed in the other hymns of the *Freudenpsalm*,[93] so a search was made for chorale-anthems among the manuscripts in the Salem Collection where such an anthem was found— Gregor's adaptation of a chorale prelude by J. P. Kellner. This elaboration on Tune 151A, the Passion

Tune 214B

Sing, o mein - e Seel - e sing - e! Sing dem Fried - e - fürst - en Dank!
Furcht-bar war der Gang der Ding - e, Doch mein Glaub - e ward nicht krank.

Trüb - sal {reg - te}{zeig - te} sich in Meng - e, Und es kam auch manch - er Schlag,
Ab - er mitt - en in Ge - dräng - e Sprach ich: "Der mich trägt und hebt,

Den man schreck - lich nenn - en mag.
Jes - us, mein Er - lös - er lebt."

Chorale, which is one of the most cherished chorales in Moravian hymnody, fits the *Freudenpsalm* text admirably; the old folio number is 63, placing the manuscript in Salem in 1783. Though I was not aware of it when the chorale-anthem was chosen for inclusion in the *Freudenpsalm*, the position of this text in relation to the other parts of the *Freudenpsalm* demands such a setting.

[XII] *Solo:* "Herr! lass die Unität"
$$(6.5 | 6.5 | 6.5 | 6.6.5) = \text{Tune 37A}$$

Of the two tunes designed to fit this meter, one (37B) contains only eight phrases: 6.5 | 6.5 | 6.5 | 6.5, so it is unsuitable for use in the *Freudenpsalm*. In Gregor's *Choralbuch*, provision for the additional six-syllable line is made in Tune 37A by the inclusion of an optional, parenthetical phrase: 6.5 | 6.5 | 6.5 | 6.(6.)5. The Salem partbooks contain neither Tune 37B nor the parenthetical phrase in an otherwise complete harmonization of Tune 37A; it can be inferred from this fact that on the 1783 Fourth of July the soloist sang the chorale tune with organ accompaniment.

[XIII] "Gruss Deinem Segen reichlich aus"
$$(8.7 | 8.7 | 8.8 | 7.7) = \text{Tune 169}$$

There were no problems encountered in selecting this tune since it is the only tune available in 1783 that fits the text.

[XIV] "Gott gib Fried in diesem Lande"
$$(8.8) = \text{Tune 23, section 1}$$

The only hymn text borrowed from the 1763 peace festival Psalms, this passage could have presented many problems because of its brevity and apparent incompleteness. However, the Salem partbooks contain a two-phrase version of Tune 23 that fits this passage exactly; the Salem Congregation apparently sang this abbreviated version of the tune as a kind of musical response.

The search for chorale tunes used in the *Freudenpsalm* was successfully completed in the summer of 1966. The only items still missing from the the *Freudenpsalm* music were the elusive recitatives and duet. After combing the Salem archives in vain, I had almost given up hope of finding those last three pieces of the *Freudenpsalm* puzzle. Two years passed, and the Fourth of July research was set aside to make room for new projects.

One day in August 1968, while browsing in the Lititz Room of the Moravian Archives in Bethlehem, Pennsylvania, I noticed a box marked "Miscellaneous Fragments," which I opened. There—at the bottom of a pile of dusty paper scraps—lay an incomplete, unlisted, unnumbered, unidentified set of manuscript parts that proved to be the musical setting of the *Danck-Psalm* sung at the 1763 peace festival in Gnadenfrey. It was from this *Danck-Psalm* that Friedrich Peter had borrowed the texts for the two recitatives and duet that were still missing from the Salem *Freudenpsalm*. With these "miscellaneous fragments" the *Freudenpsalm* could be completed and the music for the 1783 Fourth of July observance could be fully restored. Furthermore, with the discovery of the Gnadenfrey music, the one uncomfortable choice of the *Freudenpsalm* music, the setting for "Jauchzet dem HErrn" [III], could be evaluated, for the Gnadenfrey Psalm had been Peter's source of that text. The first anthem in the Gnadenfrey music, "Jauchzet dem HErrn," is a variant version of the Salem anthem[94] I had so reluctantly included in the *Freudenpsalm*; my choice was now substantiated by evidence. The search was over, the puzzle solved, but the project was not finished.

Now that the various parts of the *Freudenpsalm* could be assembled in order, the musical result must be viewed in its totality and its value assessed. Produced in such haste, the *Freudenpsalm* music could have emerged as a shapeless conglomeration of unrelated compositions, a hodgepodge of anthems and chorales haphazardly strung together to mask the sound of clinking cups and shuffling feet that accompanies a Lovefeast. What does emerge, however, is a unified musical composition that demonstrates careful planning and execution. To be sure, the peculiar requirements of a Lovefeast are met; the outer anthems [II+III and XV+XVI] accommodate the serving and removal of the Lovefeast food while the inner movements assigned to soloists and choruses allow time for its consumption, but these practical

demands are considered within the boundaries of a musically balanced structure. Friedrich Peter was a thorough musician who could not ignore his musical instincts even under the pressure of an imminent deadline; a resourceful man, he took the miscellaneous materials at hand and recycled them in order to produce a new and useful musical product:

I.	Chorale:	Everyone
II.	{ Anthem:	Chorus + Strings
III.	{ Anthem:	Chorus + Strings + Winds
IV.	*CHORALE: *Tune 230*	Congregation
V.	Recitative:	Solo
VI.	Chorale:	Everyone
VII.	Duet:	Soloists + Strings
VIII.	Chorale:	Congregation
IX.	Recitative:	Solo
X.	Chorale-Anthem	Women's Chorus + Strings
XI.	*CHORALE: *Tune 230*	Congregation
XII.	Chorale:	Solo
XIII.	Chorale:	Choruses
XIV.	Chorale:	Congregation
XV.	{ Anthem:	Chorus + Strings
XVI.	{ Anthem:	Chorus + Strings + Winds
XVII.	*CHORALE: *Tune 230*	Everyone

In reading through this list of compositions, it is immediately apparent that the recurring chorale Tune 230 [IV, XI, XVII] draws together and unifies the *Freudenpsalm* setting. Spaced at strategic intervals within the structure, the three statements of Tune 230 act as pillars upon which the weight of the composition rests. The distribution of the five anthems within the *Freudenpsalm* underscores the structural significance of Tune 230. Buttressing the first and last statements of the chorale [IV and XVII] are pairs of anthems [II+III and XV+XVI] that exhibit similar characteristics. In each pair of anthems, the first [II and XV] is a composition by Christian Gregor, setting forth the text in a simple, straightforward manner to an accompaniment of strings and organ; the second anthem in each pair [III and XVI] is an elaborate musical setting, composed or adapted by Johann Christian Geisler, in which the instrumental forces are expanded to include flutes and horns as well as strings and organ. The key schemes of the paired compositions further enhance their similarities (II + III = G minor + D major; XV+XVI = G minor-B-flat major + D major). At the center of the *Freudenpsalm* is another statement of Tune 230 [XI] preceded by a single anthem, Gregor's adaptation for women's voices with strings and organ of the chorale prelude on Tune 151A by J. P. Kellner. These three clusters, dominated by Tune 230A, are the key elements in the balanced, symmetrical organization of the *Freudenpsalm*, for which the opening chorale [I] acts as an introduction. The intervening movements that link the clusters are also arranged in an orderly fashion. Movements V through IX have their own symmetry:

Recitative   Chorale   Duet   Chorale   Recitative

and the three chorales comprising movements XII through XIV are set for progressively larger performing forces: Solo → Choruses → Congregation. In the skilled, experienced hands of Friedrich Peter, these various musical strands are woven into a tightly knit, symmetrical structure:

I ⋮ II+III+IV ⋮ V VI VII VIII IX ⋮ X XI ⋮ XII+XIII+XIV ⋮ XV+XVI+XVII

The *Freudenpsalm* thus fulfills those practical needs peculiar to a Lovefeast Service without sacrificing the current musical principles of balance and order.

Several features found in the music used in Salem on the Fourth of July in 1783 suggest areas of research that lie outside the scope of the present project. Among these are musical curiosities found in the chorale harmonizations derived from the Salem partbooks, including unusual chords, harmonic and melodic progressions, and voice leading. Particularly intriguing are the numerous parallel fifths formed by the leaping tenor and bass parts at cadence points. Though awkward and "wrong," the resulting sound is fresh and vigorous, and without doubt, intentional. These peculiar progressions occur with such frequency that they cannot be dismissed as accidents or errors; Friedrich Peter was well schooled in current harmonic practice and he would not have made such glaring mistakes unless he liked them. A thorough study of the available chorale harmonizations would add to our present limited knowledge of the harmonic techniques practiced by Moravian musicians.

Anyone with even a superficial knowledge of the Moravian anthem repertoire is aware of the fact that Moravian composers were inveterate borrowers and adapters of preexistent music (e.g., *Freudenpsalm* III and X); the use of *contrafactum* is so prevalent among Moravian musicians and so complex in its application that a competent study would occupy the attention of a team of scholars for several years in order to trace the borrowed compositions back through several generations of *contrafacta* to their original sources. A less well-known feature of Moravian music is the frequent use of musical description, several examples of which occur in the Fourth of July music. A most obvious use of descriptive writing is found in Gregor's setting of *Gelobt seyst Du* in which the text is sung to the typical chant formulae of the liturgies (see Gregor's *Choralbuch*, nos. 539A, B, and 540b-e), with a few touches of word-painting (e.g., mm. 6–8, 29–30, 43–48). To relieve the monotony of the recurring formulae, the orchestra engages in detailed musical description, depicting, among other things, rain (m. 33), wind (m. 40), lightning (mm. 41–42), and the flight of birds (mm. 70–73). Less obvious excursions into musical description take place in two anthems of the *Freudenpsalm* (XV, mm. 16–25 and XVI, mm. 65–67, 78–87). The playful side of the Moravian musical character has been ignored by researchers and warrants further investigation.

IV

Music for the Fourth of July, 1783, in Salem: An Edition

With the four exceptions noted in the editorial comments provided for each composition, this edition is based on manuscript parts contained in the Salem Congregation music and preserved in the archives of The Moravian Music Foundation in Winston-Salem, North Carolina. The score arrangement follows the order found in eighteenth-century manuscript scores in the Moravian music collections, i.e., brasses are placed at the top of the score, followed in descending order by woodwinds, the three upper string parts, voices, and finally, the continuo. Modern clefs have been substituted for soprano, alto, and tenor clefs used in the original vocal parts and the soprano clef that appears in some organ parts. At the beginning of each anthem, the parts are labeled and the initial measures are given as they appear in the original manuscript.

Since the purpose of this edition is to present as faithfully as possible the music as the Salem musicians saw it in 1783, only obvious scribal errors have been corrected in the score. Redundant accidentals and conflicting dynamic, tempo, and phrase markings have been retained; reconciliation of markings is limited to the individual part. The few editorial additions and emendations are either enclosed in brackets or represented by broken lines. Lower-case letters encircled on the score are indications that editorial changes or interpretations are discussed in the editorial notes.

Except for the Te Deum, an English translation of the German text is provided within the score for each composition; to avoid unnecessary clutter, it is placed under the original text of just one voice part. Since several of the musical sections in the Te Deum accommodate from four to six verses of text, it was felt that a translation given in its entirety at the end of the composition would be more useful and less cumbersome than a line-by-line translation on the score; the English version given here is adapted from the Moravian Hymnal (1920). Translations of various parts of the *Freudenpsalm*, which were made by

Adelaide L. Fries[1] (ALF) in 1913 have been included in this edition if they fit the musical settings; the remainder of the texts have been translated by the editor (MPG).

With the music for the Fourth of July observance assembled and transcribed, there remains one area to be explored—its performance. How did the music sound? There is no clearcut answer to such a question, of course; such factors as the number and proficiency of the performers and the quality and condition of the instruments, which bear on the answer, cannot be determined. Does the score presented here provide all the information necessary to recreate the performance? To this question there are at least partial answers. Except for the organ parts, the anthems as they appear in the score require only minor editing to prepare them for modern performance. One anthem (*Freudenpsalm* X) is supplied with an almost complete organ part, but the remainder are provided with skeletal organ parts consisting primarily of melody and figured bass that must be filled out. The figures given in florid organ parts (e.g., *Freudenpsalm* III and XVI), if followed exactly, will produce a satisfactory three-part texture in which the right hand plays the melody, doubled at the third or sixth below, and the left hand follows the bass line; only a few full chords need be supplied in cadential passages. The less-ornamented anthems, in which the instruments do little more than double the voices (e.g., *Freudenpsalm* II and XV), would benefit from a stronger organ part, its texture thickened by fuller chords. If the organist for the day followed the usual Moravian practice, he did not elaborate further on the written part, for, as Christian Gregor admonished in the preface to his *Choralbuch* (1784), organists in Moravian services were expected to avoid unseemly, virtuosic displays. The realization of the part must also take into consideration the capabilities of the Bullitschek organ used in the 1783 performance, a small one-manual instrument without pedal.[2] Having but two stops (probably an 8′ Flute and a 4′ Principal or Flute), its tonal resources would be limited to the 8′ sound and the brighter 8′ and 4′ combination. The makeshift swell mechanism[3] could provide at least four dynamic levels: 8′ (closed swell), 8′ (open swell), 8′ + 4′ (closed swell), and 8′ + 4′ (open swell); whether or not the swell could be manipulated to produce further gradations in volume is not clear from its descriptions in the Moravian records or from a study of the surviving photograph of its twin (Figure B).

The manner in which the *Freudenpsalm* chorales were performed is less certain since the text specifies only the vocal groups that are to be used in the various chorales. It is possible, of course, that the organ provided the only accompaniment for the unison singing in all the chorales; the one solo rendition of a chorale (*Freudenpsalm* XII) was undoubtedly accompanied by organ alone, since the extant harmonized version of that chorale lacks one phrase that must be present in order to set the hymn text. As one possible method of performance, the melody and figured bass version of each chorale has been included in this edition. A second possibility arises if one considers the fact that all of the chorales, with the exception of the solo chorale mentioned above, appear in the four-part harmonizations used by the instrumentalists at the time, and that their availability in the partbooks may even have influenced Friedrich Peter's decision to include them in the *Freudenpsalm*. Furthermore, it is difficult to believe that the Moravians, with their aversion to waste of any kind, would permit their instruments to lie idle while the organ carried the entire burden of accompaniment to the chorales, especially since the orderly use of those instruments would enhance the antiphonal effects Friedrich Peter was actively seeking. For these reasons, the four-part harmonizations of the chorales are also included in this edition.

If, indeed, the instruments were used to accompany the chorales, another question is posed. What did each instrument play? The harmonizations are contained in the four partbooks that are identified only by the clefs used: soprano, alto, tenor, and bass, respectively; no instrumentation is indicated. Some clues can be gleaned from the evidence at hand, however. The role played by the brass choir is easy to establish; there is ample evidence in the Salem

records, fortified by the accounts of the 1763 peace festivals in Germany, to indicate the fact that when the congregation sang, the brasses supported it. The use of the orchestra can only be surmised from the instrumentation employed in the *Freudenpsalm* anthems. The one anthem assigned to Chorus II alone uses strings and continuo (*Freudenpsalm* II) and the same group accompanies Chorus I in another anthem (*Freudenpsalm* XV); however, Chorus I is more often fortified by the full orchestra of flutes, horns, strings, and continuo (*Freudenpsalm* III and XVI). Bearing in mind the Moravians' predilection for the antiphonal performance of chorales, the large body of evidence confirming the use of brasses to support congregational singing, and a less convincing case for the assignment of strings and continuo to Chorus I and full orchestra to Chorus II, the performance of the *Freudenpsalm* chorales could have encompassed the following groups:

Chorus I	Chorus II	Congregation ("Gem.")	Everyone ("Alle")
+	+	+	+
flutes	strings	brasses	brasses
horns	continuo		flutes
strings			horns
continuo			strings
			continuo

That the harmonizations exist only in books containing a single part creates certain restrictions on the assignment of parts to the various instruments within these groups. Since it is doubtful that partbooks would be exchanged during the performance, the players must have been assigned one of the four parts to play for all of the chorales contained in the *Freudenpsalm*. The most obvious factor to be considered in the assignment of parts is the range of the particular instrument. The brass choir was organized to perform just such harmonizations and the distribution of parts presents no problem; the four members of the string section can easily accommodate the complete harmonization also. The incomplete wind section poses special problems, however. The flutes are capable of playing the soprano and alto parts of those chorales in which they would participate if the scoring plan offered above is followed but, in other chorales in the *Freudenpsalm*, the alto part lies below the flute's range. Therefore, only in the event that the scoring followed the suggested order could the flutes have played in unison with the violins. A second solution that might prove to be more satisfactory than the one just offered is based on the treatment of the flutes in the anthems of the *Freudenpsalm*. In the anthems, the total range covered by the flutes is:

but their parts usually lie within these ranges:

Flute I:    Flute II:

and their musical lines consist primarily of doubling the two violin parts, either at the unison, if the strings are playing in the ranges just given, or at the octave above, if the strings fall below these ranges; additional evidence of the octave doubling appears in the flute parts added in 1788[4] to one of the anthems appearing in the *Freudenpsalm* [II], which consist entirely of octave doublings of the first and second violin parts. Thus an alternative to the flutes' performance of the soprano and alto parts of the chorales at written pitch could be the transposition of those same parts to the octave above.

Disposition of the horn parts must take into account not only range but also the restrictions imposed by valveless instruments (Figure A) with their limited number of available pitches. The soprano part lies outside the range of the instrument and the bass part could not have been played on the horns used in 1783. This leaves the alto and tenor parts as the only possible assignments to be given to the horns. At least two crooks (G and D) were required to perform the anthems in the Fourth of July music, and by changing from one to the other as the key of the chorale demands, together with some utilization of hand-stopping, the horn players could have per-

formed satisfactorily the alto and tenor parts of the chorales that would be assigned to them in the suggested scoring plan.

By applying the suggestions given above—the utilization and division of the instrumental forces into groups and the distribution of parts among those groups—to the simple, four-part harmonizations given in this edition, the chorales enhance the festive character of the *Freudenpsalm*. The opening chorale [I], edited for modern performance according to the suggested scoring plan, serves as an illustration; in the arrangement that appears on the following pages, trumpets are substituted for the treble and alto trombones of the old *Posaunenchor* and the horn parts are transposed to conform to modern usage.

Translated by
Adelaide L. Fries (1913)

I. Chorale

Tune 56
harmonized by JFP
arranged by MPG

A faithful edition of the music performed in Salem on the Fourth of July, 1783, is an unfinished product, for to present Moravian music as a separate entity is to distort history. Music was as essential as food and drink to eighteenth-century Moravians, and it cannot be extracted from its surroundings without losing much of its significance. The day must be recreated and the music placed in its proper context. In attempting to recapture that day, one must turn again to Johann Friedrich Peter who, though never mentioned by name in the records of the day, is the central figure, involved in every phase of the observance. As protocollist, he attended and participated in the planning sessions held by the Elders Conference during the week preceding the celebration, and he recorded those plans in the minutes of the meetings. As archivist, he searched the accounts of the 1763 peace festivals held in Germany, selecting and adapting passages that fit the needs of the Salem Peace Festival. As poet, he may have composed some of the special hymn texts for the *Freudenpsalm*. As copyist, he helped to prepare copies of the *Freudenpsalm* text for distribution to the congregation. As musical director, he compiled, rehearsed, and directed the musical portions of the observance. And, finally as diarist, he wrote the official description of the celebration from the first sounds of the trombones at dawn to the twilight pronouncement of the Benediction, preserving a complete record of the day's events.

By combining Friedrich Peter's recollections as he recorded them in the Salem Diary with the music as he planned and directed it, the sights and sounds of the Day of Solemn Thanksgiving can be restored:

Diarium / der / Gemeine / in / Salem / 1783.[a]
Julius 1783.
* * *

Diary of the Congregation in Salem, 1783
July, 1783.
* * *

d. 4. feyerten wir[b] der Verordnung der Regierung des hiesigen Staats zu folge das Friedens-Dankfest wegen der in diesen Landen wiederhergestellten Ruhe. Die Gemeine[c] wurde mit Posaunen geweckt, u. zu Anfang der Predigt wurde[d] das Te Deum unter Posaunenschall fröhlich angestimmt.

the 4th. In compliance with the decree of the government of this State, we observed the Day of Solemn Thanksgiving for the reestablished peace in this land. The congregation was wakened with trombones, and at the beginning of the Preaching Service, the Te Deum was sung with the joyous pealing of the trombones.

[a]An almost identical description of the Fourth of July observance appears in *Extract des Diarii der Gemeinen in der Wachau 1783*, an annual report of newsworthy events occurring in the Moravian settlements in Wachovia.
[b]*Extract* inserts the phrase: "an allen unsern Orten (in all our settlements)."
[c]*Extract* inserts the phrase: "in Salem."
[d]*Extract* omits the word "wurde."

Das Te Deum Laudamus

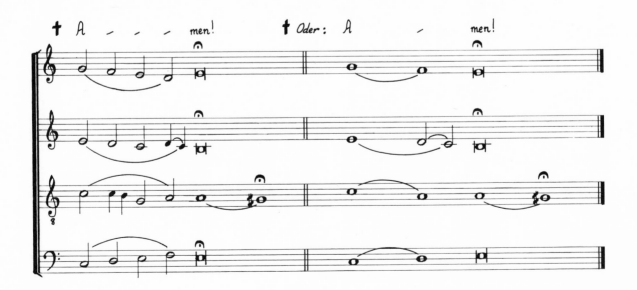

Das Te Deum Laudamus

Lord God, Thy praise we sing, / To Thee our thanks we bring;

Thou Father of eternity, / Both heaven and earth do worship Thee;
To Thee all angels loudly cry, / The heavens and all the powers on high:
Cherubs and seraphs all rejoice / singing with ever louder voice:

Holy is our Lord God! / Holy is our Lord God!
Holy is our Lord God! / The Lord of Sabaoth!

With splendor of Thy glory spread, / Are heaven and earth replenished.
The apostles' holy company, / The prophets' fellowship praise Thee,
The noble and victorious host / Of martyrs makes of Thee their boast.
The holy Church in every place / Throughout the earth, exalts Thy praise,
Thee, Father, God on heaven's throne, / Thy only and beloved Son,
The Holy Ghost and Comforter / The Church doth worship and revere.

O Christ, Thou glorious King, we own / Thee to be God's eternal Son:
Thou, undertaking in our room, / Didst not abhor the Virgin's womb.
The pains of death o'ercome by Thee, / Made heaven to all believers free.
At God's right hand Thou hast Thy seat / And in Thy Father's glory great.
And we believe the day's decreed / When Thou shalt judge the quick and dead.
Promote, we pray, Thy servants' good, / Redeemed with Thy most precious blood:

Among Thy saints let us ascend / To glory that shall never end.

Thy people with salvation crown! / Bless those, O Lord, that are Thine own.
Govern Thy Church, and, Lord, advance / Forever Thine inheritance.

From day to day, O Lord, do we / Highly exalt and honor Thee.

Vouchsafe, O Lord, we humbly pray, / To keep us safe from sin this day:
O Lord have mercy on us all! / Have mercy on us when we call:
Thy mercy, Lord, to us dispense, / According to our confidence.

Lord, we have put our trust in Thee, / Confounded let us never be.
Amen!

—adapted from the *Hymnal and Liturgies of the Moravian Church* (1920), pp. 170–71.

Die Losung am 20. Jan.—
als an welchem Tage
Friedens-Praeliminarien
unterzeichnet worden—:
Der Gott Jacob ist Schuz
gab Gelegenheit den 46.
Psalm, aus welchem sie
genommen ist, zum Text
der Predigt zu nehmen,
über welchen Br. Benzien
von dem Gott schuldigen
Dank für den wiederher-
gestellten Frieden und
der rechten Anwendung
desselben zu desto unge-
störterem Genuss des
Friedens Gottes im Herzen
redete, u. darauf für einen
dauerhaften Frieden zu einem
beständigen Glück hiesigen
Landes und dessen Regierung
den Segen Gottes erbat. Den
Beschluss der Predigt machte
der musikalische Gesang: Ehre
sey Gott in der Höhe, &

The Losung for January 20—
the day on which the Peace
Preliminaries were signed—:
*The God of Jacob is our
Refuge* gave rise to the
suggestion that the 46th
Psalm, from which it is
taken, be selected as the
text for the sermon, during
which Br. Benzien delivered
a discourse concerning the
gratitude owed to God for
the restored peace and its
proper application to the
more quiet enjoyment of
Godly peace in our hearts,
and then, for the sake of a
permanent peace, he asked
God's blessing for the continued good fortune of this
land and its government. At
the close of the sermon was
sung the anthem: Glory to
God in the Highest, &

Ehre sey Gott in der Höhe

Nachmittags um 2 Uhr war ein fröhliches Lmhl., dabey der unten beygefügte *Freudenpsalm* mit dankbaren Herzen und Munde angestimmt wurde.

In the afternoon about 2 o'clock, there was a joyous Lovefeast, during which the appended *Psalm of Joy* was sung with thankful hearts and mouths.

Freudenpsalm
der Gemeine in Salem
zum Friedens-Dankfeste.
d. 4. Juli 1783

[I. Chorale]

Chorus I.

Chorus II.

[II. Anthem]

[III. Anthem]

[*IV. Chorale*]

Gem.

Freud-en-voll lasst uns nun sing - en, Und uns-erm Gott Dank-opf-er

Full of — joy our hearts are sing - ing, And to our Gott thank-off-'rings

bring - en Für Sein-e gross-e — Wund-er-that! Schreck-en-voll auf

bring - ing For His great mir-a-cle of peace! Far and — wide the

[V.] *Recitativ.*

Welt, der Bog-en, Schwerdt und Schild zer-bricht, Spiess-e zer-schlägt, und Wag-en mit Feu-er ver-
earth, the ar-row, sword and shield He breaks, split-ting the spear; and burn-ing with fire the

brenn-et. Das Land ist all-ent-halb-en jäm-mer-lich ver-wüst-et, und die
char-iot. The land now lies in waste pil-laged and rav-aged, and the

Häus-er sind zer-riss-en; weil nun die El-end-en ver-stör-et werd-en, und die Arm-en seuf-zen, will
dwell-ings torn a-sun-der. For now the need-y who en-dure op-pres-sion, and the poor who sor-row, shall

ich auf, spricht der HErr, will ich auf, spricht der HErr: All-e Krieg-er
I rise, saith the Lord, shall I rise, saith the Lord: On the bat-tle-

müss-en die Händ-e lass-en sink-en, all-e Krieg-er müss-en die Händ-e lass-en
fields let all sold-iers drop their weap-ons, on the bat-tle-fields let all sold-iers drop their

sink-en, denn ich will auf, spricht der HErr, sie müss-en die Händ-e lass-en sink-en.
weap-ons, for I shall rise, saith the Lord, all sold-iers now must drop their weap-ons.

[VI. Chorale]

Gem.

Du — bist — GOtt, | Du bist GOtt, | Jes - u, du Ge - kreuz - ig - ter! | Gott - es Lamm, für
Thou — art — God, | Thou art God, | Jes - us Christ, the Cruc - i - fied! | Lamb of God who

uns ge - schlacht - et, | Du bist all - er Herr - en HErr! | Legst - auch den, der Dich ver - acht - et,
came to — save us, | Lord of Lords — who for us died! | Once des - pised, He now doth — raise us

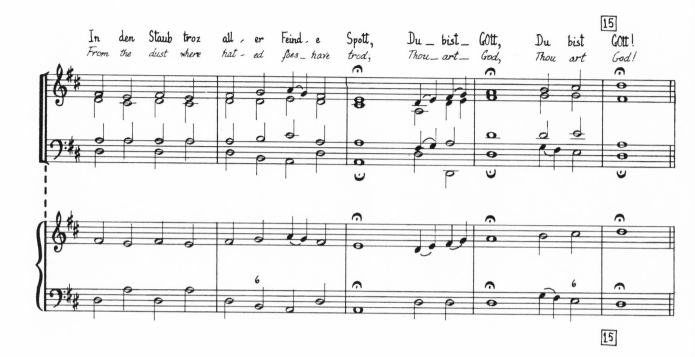

[VII.] *Duetto.*

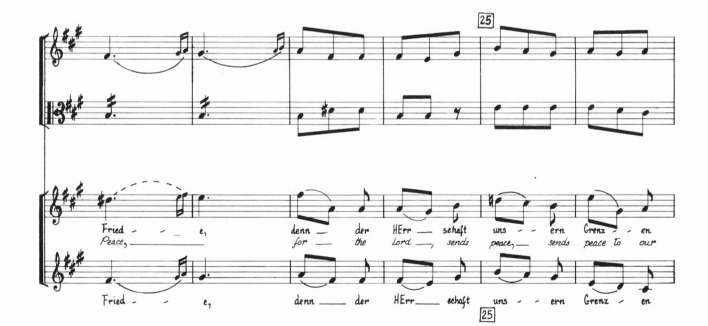

[VIII. Chorale]

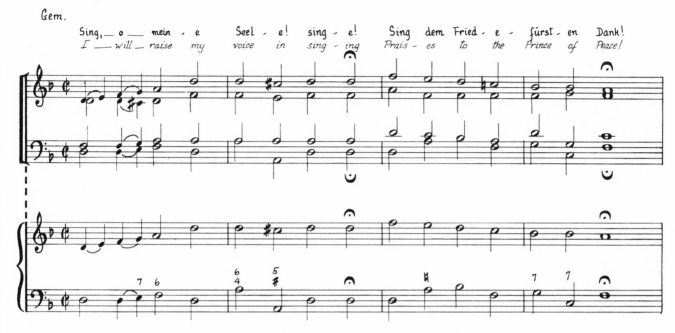

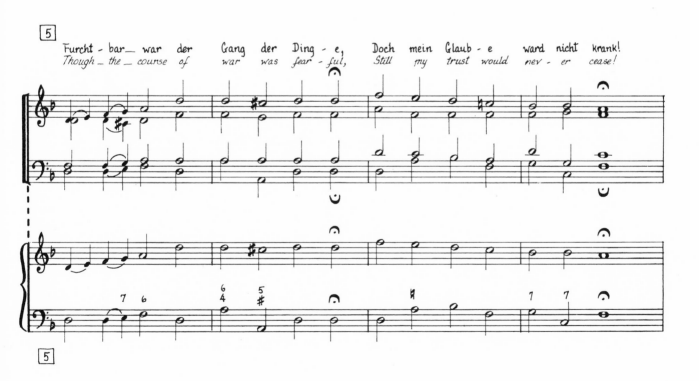

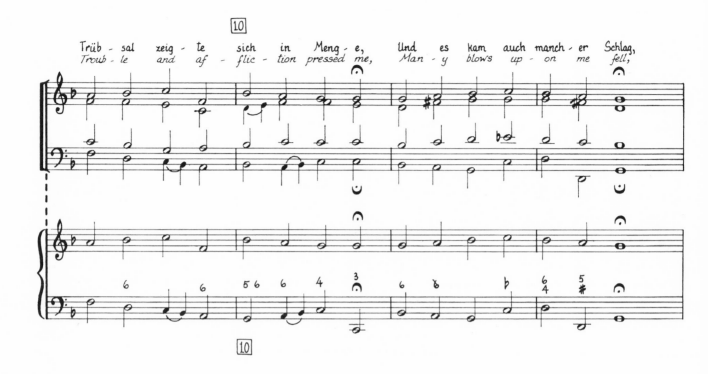

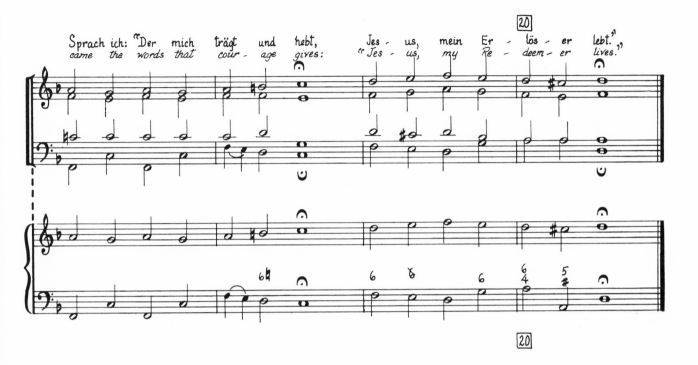

[IX.] *Recitativ.*

[X. Chorale-Anthem] Arietta.

[XI. Chorale]

[XII. Chorale]

Solo.

[XIII. Chorale]

Beyde Chöre.

[XIV. Chorale]

[XV. Anthem]

[Chorale-Response]

[XVI. Anthem]

[XVII. Chorale]

Alle.

Abends gegen 8 Uhr versammlete sich die Gemeine wider auf dem Saal. Der Chorus musicus stimmte an: Gelobet seyst Du, der du sizest über Cherubim &

In the evening toward 8 o'clock, the Congregation again assembled in the *Saal*. The chorus of musicians performed: Praise be to Thee, who enthroned above the Cherubim &

Gelobt seyst du, der du sizest über Cherubim

worauf die Gemeine vor dem Gemeinhause einen Kreis formirte, und von da mit Musik und dem abwechselnden Gesang zweyer Chöre in Procession durch die Hauptstrassen des Orts, welcher illuminiret war, ging; und nachdem sie vor dem Gemeinhause wieder einen Kreis formiret hatte mit dem Segen des HErrn zu Ruhe entlassen wurde. Die Herzen waren von dem sanften Frieden Gottes angethan, welcher den ganzen Tag und sonderlich bey der Procession auf eine hinnehmende Weise waltete, und der durch eine tiefe Stille von aussen, damit selbst die Luft correspondirte, lieblich aus-gedrückt wurde.[a]

whereupon the congregation formed a circle in front of the *Gemein-haus,* and from there, with instru-mental music and the antiphonal singing of the two Choirs, they walked in procession through the main streets of the town which was illuminated; and after they had again formed a circle before the *Gemeinhaus,* they were dis-missed to rest with the Lord's Blessing. Hearts were filled with the gentle Godly peace that had prevailed the entire day and was felt in a particularly compelling manner during the procession; this was expressed all around us by a deep silence, for even the wind was still.

[a]*Extract* adds: "Dieser Festtag wurde in Bethabara auf ähnlich Weise begangen" ("This holiday was celebrated in Bethabara in similar fashion").

Editorial Commentary

The principal sources consulted in the preparation of the music edition and the accompanying commentary fall into four categories: texts, musical settings, music manuscripts, and supplementary sources.

Texts

Anthems. / The German Bible is the source for identification of the scriptural passages that comprise the anthem texts.

Chorales. / GG=GESANGBUCH ZUM GEBRAUCH DER EVANGELISCHEN BRÜDERGEMEINEN (Barby, 1778). The official Moravian hymnal in use in 1783, the GESANGBUCH is a collection of hymn texts compiled by Christian Gregor to replace the many and diverse hymnals published by the Moravians during the previous forty years. In the citations, the symbol GG is followed by the hymn number and the number of the stanza from which the text is taken.

Musical Settings

Anthems. / Names of composers and/or arrangers are given as they appear in the music manuscripts and catalogs listed below. If there is disagreement among the sources, all the attributions and their sources are given. The dates in parentheses refer to the earliest known use of the musical setting, as recorded by Johannes Herbst in his collection of manuscript scores.

Chorales. / Since the tunebook used by Salem organists in 1783 has not survived, this edition relies on the first two sources listed below for the melody and figured bass version of the chorales.

GrC=the so-called Grimm CHORALBUCH, a manuscript collection of chorale melodies with figured bass thought to have been compiled by Johann Daniel Grimm ca. 1755 for use by Herrnhut organists in accompanying congregational singing. The original manuscript is preserved in Archiv der Brüderunität, Herrnhut, East Germany; a microfilm copy is housed in The Moravian Music Foundation, Winston-Salem, North Carolina. The tunes are classified by hymn meters, and each of the 570 classes is assigned a number. Many of the classifications (*Arten*) contain several different tunes, each of which is identified by its own letter added to the basic number, e.g., "Art 151A" is the Passion chorale "O Haupt voll Blut und Wunden." Although this collection was not recognized as the official choralebook for the Moravian congregations, it served as a model for subsequent collections and its classification and numbering systems have continued in use to the present day.

GC=CHORAL-BUCH, ENTHALTEND ALLE ZU DEM GESANGBUCHE DER EVANGELISCHEN BRÜDER-GEMEINEN VOM JAHRE 1778 GEHÖRIGE MELODIEN (Leipzig, 1784). Compiled by Christian Gregor as a companion to his 1778 hymnal, this is the first printed Moravian choralebook. Gregor's purpose in compiling the tunebook, as he states in its preface, was to standardize the tunes and their harmonizations and to update Grimm's choralebook. Gregor reduced the number of melody types from 570 to 260, containing over 500 separate melodies. He retained the old classification and numbering system, but omitted those numbers whose tunes had been used as settings for hymns that had not survived the post-Zinzendorf revision of Moravian hymnody. Within the various classifications that remained, Gregor discarded some old tunes and added sixty new melodies. In noting the melodic and harmonic differences between the two versions of each tune given in this edition, it should be kept in mind that the Salem musicians did not receive copies of the new printed choralebook until 5 July 1785—two years after the Fourth of July observance—but the harmonized versions in the partbooks described below were familiar to them. In the event of disagreement, the latter should be considered the better source.

SB=A set of four partbooks containing SATB (soprano, alto, tenor, bass) harmonizations of chorales for the use of the *Posaunenchor* or brass choir. An entry in the Musical Accounts for 24 April 1781[1] lists the expenditure "An Choral-Buchel f. die Posaunen einzubinde," establishing the existence of the partbooks well before the 1783 Fourth of July observance. The four books, labeled according to range rather than instrumentation, are preserved in The Moravian Music Foundation, Winston-Salem, North Carolina.

Music Manuscripts

S=THE SALEM CONGREGATION COLLECTION. The basic library of concerted music intended for use in worship services, the Salem Collection consists of folios, each of which contains vocal and instrumental parts for several compositions. During the first thirty years of its existence, the collection grew to 200 folios containing over 500 compositions; by 1783, the library must have contained at least 101 folios for that is the highest number assigned to any of the compositions used in the Fourth of July observance. When the collection was reorganized in 1808, some folios were discarded and others were renumbered. The collection is now arranged in the order established in 1808. In identifying the manuscripts used for this edition, the collection symbol (s) is followed by the present folio number and the secondary number that is assigned to an individual composition within the folio, e.g., "Jauchzet dem HErrn" (*Freudenpsalm* III), the third anthem in Folio 26, is identified as "s 26.3." Following this identification, if the folio is one of those that were renumbered during the 1808 reorganization, the old number—the number in use in 1783—is given in parentheses. Consequently, the full identification of "Jauchzet dem HErrn" is: s 26.3 (old No. 101).

SS=THE SALEM SISTERS' COLLECTION. A separate library within the Salem Congregation music for the use of the women singers ("das Schwestern-Sänger Chor"),[2] this collection contains the vocal parts (often—and inexplicably—including the bass part) for the concerted anthems performed during Moravian worship services. Since there is no mention of this collection before the cataloging project of 1808, it is possible that it was formed at that time as a separate entity. No attempt was made to coordinate the numerical arrangement of this collection with the larger, more complete Salem Congregation Collection. As in the Salem Collection, each folio contains the parts for several compositions and the same numbering procedure is adopted for individual compositions within a folio, e.g., the anthem "Jauchzet dem HErrn" bears the number ss 3.3 in the Sisters' library.

H=THE JOHANNES HERBST COLLECTION. In 1811 Johannes Herbst brought his private library of manuscript scores to Salem where, after his death in 1812, it was deposited in the church archives. Although it is not a part of the Salem Congregation music, the Herbst Collection has been an invaluable source in this edition. Its 473 manuscripts, containing over one thousand anthems and arias for use in Moravian worship services, provide a historical survey of the Moravian art-music tradition from its beginnings in Christian Gregor's initial Lovefeast Psalms through a half century of growth. In addition to his copies of the music, Herbst's annotations giving names of composers or compilers, dates and events for which compositions were first prepared are the most complete and accurate sources of such information yet discovered.

L=THE LITITZ CONGREGATION COLLECTION. This library of musical parts contains the music used for worship services held in the Moravian Church in Lititz, Pennsylvania; the collection is now housed in the Moravian Archives in Bethlehem, Pennsylvania. It is in this collection that the parts of the *Freuden-psalm* lacking in the Salem Collection were found.

Supplementary Sources

Of the numerous documents consulted during the preparation of this study, the catalogs of the various music collections and the descriptions of the peace festivals held in the German Moravian settlements following the close of the Seven Years' War in 1763 are cited most frequently in the following notes. For the sake of clarity and conciseness, the lengthy titles of these sources have been abbreviated in the following manner:

Catalogs.[3]

1. ANMERCKUNGEN . . . 1808 = ANMERCKUNGEN BEYM DURCHSEHEN DER MUSICALIEN DER GEMEINE IN SALEM. MART. 1808 (Observations in connection with the review of the congregation music in Salem. March, 1808), compiled by Johannes Reuz (1752–

1810). The ANMERCKUNGEN contains the only surviving list of Salem Congregation manuscripts arranged according to the old numbering system.[4] To the left of each number, the names of composers represented by compositions in the folder are entered; following the number are comments concerning the condition of the manuscript and, at times, Reuz's estimation of the quality of the music. Compositions are rarely mentioned by title in the ANMERCKUNGEN so that the identification of specific pieces is difficult.

2. CATALOGUS . . . IN ALPHABETISCHER ORDNUNG . . . 1808 = CATALOGUS DER GEMEIN MUSICKEN WELCHE DER GEMEINE IN SALEM GEHÖREN, IN ALPHABETISCHER ORDNUNG: VERFERTIGET IM JAHR 1808. This listing of the Salem Congregation Collection (s), arranged alphabetically by title, was begun by Reuz in 1808 and continued throughout the nineteenth century. The composer's name precedes each title, which is followed by its new folio and secondary number.

3. CATALOGUS . . . NACH ORDNUNG DER NUMMERN . . . 1808 = CATALOGUS DER GEMEIN MUSICKEN, WELCHE DER GEMEINE IN SALEM GEHÖREN, NACH ORDNUNG DER NUMMERN VERFERTIGET IM JAHR 1808. A companion to the alphabetical catalog, this volume contains a listing of the Salem Congregation Collection according to folio number; the individual compositions within each folio are listed by secondary number. Composers' names are placed in the left margin and, in the right margin, the instrumentation for each composition is given.

4. CATALOGUS . . . FÜR DAS SCHWESTERN-SÄNGER CHOR . . . IN ALPHABETISCHER ORDNUNG . . . 1808 = CATALOGUS DER GEMEIN MUSICKEN FÜR DAS SCHWESTERN-SÄNGER CHOR DER GEMEINE IN SALEM IN ALPHABETISCHER ORDNUNG VERFERTIGET IM JAHR 1808. This manuscript, containing an alphabetical listing of the Sisters' Collection (ss) by title, is defective; pages containing titles beginning with the letters A through L are extant. The format of the catalog follows that used in the alphabetical catalog of the Salem Congregation Collection.

5. CATALOGUS . . . FÜR DAS SCHWESTERN-SÄNGER CHOR . . . NACH ORDNUNG DER NUMMERN . . . 1808 = CATALOGUS DER GEMEIN MUSICKEN FÜR DAS SCHWESTERN-SÄNGER CHOR DER GEMEINE IN SALEM NACH ORDNUNG DER NUMMERN VERFERTIGET IM JAHR 1808. This catalog follows the general format of the numerical catalog of the Salem Congregation Collection, but it does not list instrumentation for compositions.

Descriptions of Peace Festivals.

1. NO. IV. BEYLAGE ZUR XIITEN WOCHE 1763 . . . HERRNHUTH = NO. IV. BEYLAGE ZUR XIITEN WOCHE 1763. BESCHREIBUNG DER FEYER DES FRIEDENS-DANCK-FESTES DER GEMEINE IN HERRNHUTH DEN 21TEN MART. 1763. This manuscript contains a detailed description of the peace celebration held in Herrnhut at the end of the Seven Years' War. Copies sent to Moravian settlements in America are preserved in the Moravian Archives in Bethlehem, Pennsylvania, and Winston-Salem, North Carolina.

2. NO. VI. BEYLAGE ZUR XITEN WOCHE 1763 = NO. VI. BEYLAGE ZUR XITEN WOCHE 1763. FÜNFTE SAMMLUNG VON GEMEIN-NACHRICHTEN ENTHALTEND I. DIE DIARIA AUS UNSERN TEUTSCHEN GEMEINEN MENS MART. 1763. A report of activities in German Moravian congregations other than Herrnhut, this manuscript contains descriptions of the 1763 peace festivals held in Barby, Niesky, Gnadenberg, and Gnadenfrey. Copies are preserved in the Moravian Archives in Bethlehem, Pennsylvania, and Winston-Salem, North Carolina.

DAS TE DEUM LAUDAMUS

Also performed at the peace festivals held in Gnadenfrey on 13 March 1763 at the first (8 A.M.) meeting; in Gnadenberg on 20 March 1763 at the evening service; and in Barby, Herrnhut, and Niesky on 21 March 1763 at the first (8 A.M.) gatherings. Accounts of these events mention the use of trombone accompaniment for the congregational singing.

Sources

Text. | GG 1612; translation adapted from the Moravian Hymnal (1920) by MPG.

Tune / GC Art 235A.[5]

Harmonization. / SB no. 139. Parts: soprano, alto, tenor, bass.

Since the description of the performance of the Te Deum on the Fourth of July specifically mentions the use of brass accompaniment, only the transcription of the harmonization contained in the partbooks is given. Each system contains the musical setting of a verse of the text; intermediate barlines separate the half verses, which, according to Moravian custom, were sung alternately by the men and the women of the congregation,[6] a tradition at variance with the Lutheran practice of alternating choir and congregation.[7]

EHRE SEY GOTT IN DER HÖHE

Also performed at the peace festival in Herrnhut on 21 March 1763 as the third anthem in the *Danck- und Freudenpsalm* presented during the afternoon (2 P.M.) Lovefeast.[8]

Sources

Text. / Luke 2:14, adapted and translated by MPG.

Musical Setting. / Christian Gregor (1760[9]/1763[10]).

Music Manuscripts.
   1. S 175.4[11] (old No. 33 and old No. 25 [?]). Parts: Canto 1[mo], Canto II, Alto; Violino Primo, Violino Secondo, Viola, Basso. This manuscript presently contains two sets of string parts prepared by two different copyists. One set of parts uses the tempo marking *"Lebhaft"* while the other is marked *"Allegro"*; in the latter set, the anthem is followed by the chorale *"Die Gottesseraphim,"* a favorite Christmas hymn.[12]
   2. S 168[13] (old No. 5).[14] Parts: Canto Primo, Canto Secondo, Alto, Basso; Tromba 1, Tromba 2, Flauto Trav. 1, Flauto Trav. 2; Organo. Each vocal part is labeled *"Chor I"* and contains the tempo marking *"Lebhaft."* The Organo part, prepared by the same copyist, does not have an original tempo mark, but two different markings, apparently added at different times by different scribes, now appear on the Organo

part. The earlier of the two markings, *"Moderato,"* has been partially obscured by the subsequent addition of *"Allegretto."* The flute and trumpet parts are in Johannes Herbst's hand and are identical to the parts filed with the score in his collection (H 22.3). Each of the wind parts contains his notation *"Zum Friedens- fest am 21. Mart. 1763,"* and the tempo marking *"Lebhaft, doch mässig"*; included on the same page are the parts for three anthems from the Herrnhut *Danck- und Freudenpsalm*: nos. 1, 3 (*Ehre sey Gott in der Höhe*), and 4. The wind parts are obvious replacements for the lacking wind parts listed in the numerical catalog under S 175 (see note 11, p. 209); they may have been contributed to the Salem Collection by Johannes Herbst after his arrival in Salem in 1811.[15]
   3. SS 92.[16] Parts: Canto Primo, Canto Secondo, Basso. All parts are labeled *"Choro II"*; the Basso part also includes the notation *"Tutti. Allegro."* These parts are significantly different from the vocal parts in S 175 and S 168. The initial rests in each part make no allowance for the fourteen-measure orchestral intro- duction; the numbering of rests begins with the en- trance of the voices. Only the music for mm. 19–22, 26–28, 30, 34–51, and 53–56 is given in these *Choro II* parts.
   4. H 22.3. Score: voices and strings. Parts: Tromba 1, Tromba 2, Flauto Trav. 1, Flauto Trav. 2.[17]

Since none of the manuscripts listed above contains a full set of parts, completeness of parts within the various performing divisions has been a major factor in deciding which manuscript is to be considered the basic source for each of those divisions. Of all the manuscripts available to the Salem musicians in 1783, only S 168 now contains the four vocal parts and, therefore, this edition uses that manuscript as the primary source for the vocal group. Though incomplete, the parts for a second chorus, which are found in SS 92, have been incorporated since it is probable that the two choruses available for the *Freudenpsalm* performance at the afternoon Lovefeast on the Fourth of July would have been present and participating in the morning Preaching Service as well. Those passages in the anthem in which *Choro II* joins are indicated by the use of double stems and the labeling and enclosure of the passages in brackets; stems have been provided for the missing alto part.

The Organo part is based on its one manuscript source, s 168. The copyist gave little attention to the placement of the figures between the staves; they often appear to lie in a straight line so that it is difficult to tell at a glance whether they refer to the melody or to the bass line. In this edition, the traditional figures (6̸3, 6̸4, etc.) have been placed near the bass staff while the single numbers (3, 6, ♯, etc.) have been located near either the upper or lower staff, according to the musical context.

The string parts are derived from the two sets now filed in s 175, and the trumpet and flute parts are transcribed from Herbst's identical copies found in s 168 and H 22.3. Discrepancies between the various manuscripts are cited below; it will be noted that H 22.3 and s 175.4 appear to be in accord on most points in question, while s 168 and ss 92 often agree on a slightly different version. Markings that appear in some, but not all of the manuscripts are enclosed in parentheses; editorial additions are placed in brackets.

(a) Flute I, m. 3 =

See Flute I, m. 17 and Violin I, mm. 3 and 17.

(b) The complete text is written above the melodic line of the Organo part (s 168).

(c) s 168, Basso, m. 32: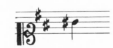

(d) s 168, Canto II, m. 34:

agreeing with ♯ in the Organo part.

s 175 and Herbst 22.3, Canto II, m. 34:

agreeing with Flute II and Violin II.

(e) In s 175 and Herbst 22.3, Canto II, m. 46 reads:

FREUDENPSALM

[I. Chorale]

Sources

Text. / Source unknown; ALF, trans.

Tune. / GC Art 56.[18]

   Harmonization. / SB no. 38. Parts: soprano, alto, tenor, bass.

[II. Anthem]

A different setting of this text was performed at the peace festival held in Herrnhut on 21 March 1763 at the afternoon Lovefeast.

Sources

Text. / Psalm 118:24; MPG, trans.

Musical Setting. / Christian Gregor (1761);[19] the second part of the bipartite anthem "Zion hörts und ist froh—Denn dis ist der Tag."

Music Manuscripts.

   1. s 107.2 (old No. 53). Parts: Canto Primo, Canto Secondo, Alto, Canto Basso; Viol⁰ Primo, Viol⁰ Sec., Viola, Basso; Organo. The vocal parts contain only the music for the second part of the bipartite anthem, beginning with "Denn dis ist der Tag"; thirteen measures of rest are indicated for the first part, with the beginning and end of the corresponding text written under the rests: "Zion hörts ——— fröhlich." On each vocal part, a flag is drawn in red ink through the staff to mark the beginning of the second part of the anthem. By observing the flag that eliminates the first word of the text, "Denn" ("For"), the second part becomes a separate anthem, complete and independent in both text and music. It should be noted, however, that the text begins "*Dis* ist *der* Tag," differing from the *Freudenpsalm* text that begins "*Das* ist *ein* Tag."

The string parts and the Organo part, all of which contain the music for both parts of the composition, bear the title "Zion hörts—Denn *dis* ist *der* Tag." However, at the beginning of the second section, each of these parts is marked with a red flag and, in addition, a notation (also in red ink) has been added in script closely resembling J. F. Peter's writing: "*Das* ist *ein* tag"—the wording found in the *Freudenpsalm* text.

2. ss 2.10. Parts: Canto Primo, Canto Secondo, Canto Alto, Canto Basso. There are two complete sets of vocal parts in this manuscript; both sets contain the music for both sections of the composition. The first set of parts, copied on full-size (ca. 8 × 13) sheets, are unlabeled; the second set, on half-sheets (ca. 6½ × 8) are labeled as above, and each part contains the notation "*Choro II.*" There is no mark separating the two sections of the composition and there is further confusion in the wording of the text beginning the second section. The Canto Primo part in both sets, entering before the other vocal parts, begins with the text "Denn *das* ist *der* Tag" but when the other voices join with it on the repetition of the phrase, the wording becomes "*Dis* ist *der* Tag," in agreement with the vocal parts of s 107.2, but at variance with the *Freudenpsalm* text.

3. H 14.2. Score.

In this edition, the text as it is found in the *Freudenpsalm* and as it is indicated by the cue marks on the instrumental parts in s 107.2 is followed, i.e., "*Das* ist *ein* Tag." The primary manuscript source for the musical setting is s 107.2, not only because it contains a complete set of parts but also because the added notations mentioned above strongly suggest that these parts were used in the Fourth of July performance. Parentheses are used to denote markings that appear in some, but not all, of the manuscript copies. Brackets indicate editorial additions, including the initial rests that compensate for the lacking quarter-note value that would result if the flagged indications were followed faithfully.

ⓐ   Violin I, m. 7 =

See "Dass in unserm Lande," prepared by the same copyist (*Freudenpsalm* XV, m. 31, note ⓖ).

ⓑ   s 107.2, Violin II, m. 17:

[III. Anthem]

Also performed at the peace festival in Gnadenfrey on 13 March 1763.

Sources

Text. / Psalms 98:4,6; 103:20,21; 96:11,12; 66:4; II.Moses 15:1; MPG, trans. With some indicated omissions, the text is given in the description of the Gnadenfrey peace festival.[20]

Musical Setting. / An adaptation of Karl Heinrich Graun's *Te Deum*, 1: "Te Deum laudamus," by Johann Christian Geisler (1763).

Music Manuscripts.

1. s 26.3 (old No. 101).[21] Parts: Canto Primo, Canto Secondo, Canto Alto, Canto Basso; Corno Primo, Corno Secondo; Flauto Traverso Primo, Flauto Traverso Secondo; Violino Primo, Violino Secondo, Viola, Basso; Organo.

2. ss 3.3.[22] "Geisler aus Grauns Tod Jesu [!]." Parts: Canto Primo, Canto Secondo, Canto Alto, Canto Basso.

3. L 441.1.[23] Parts: Canto Primo, Canto Secondo, Tenore, Basso; Violino Secondo, Viola. With the exception of a few octave transpositions to accommodate the vocal range, the Tenore part is the same as the Canto Alto part in the Salem manuscripts.

Although the three manuscripts are based on the same model, there are major differences between the Salem manuscripts and the Lititz manuscript. In the Lititz setting, the text is identical to the *Freudenpsalm* text filed with the Salem Diary; the Salem versions not only substitute words and phrases not found in the *Freudenpsalm* text, but also omit portions of it. Consequently, the Lititz setting is twenty measures longer than the Salem composition and contains some different phrase markings and note values to accommodate its text.

The Salem manuscripts were used as the basis for this edition since, in all probability, the musicians performed from those parts during the Fourth of July observance;[24] all notes and markings given in normal size are taken from the Salem parts as is the text that appears below the individual vocal parts. The *Freudenpsalm* text as it appears in the Lititz manuscript, together with its translation, is placed above the Canto Primo part; notes and phrase markings peculiar to the Lititz version are indicated by smaller notes and thin, broken lines (see mm. 30, 46–50, 58, 59, 81–90). The two passages in the Lititz setting that are not included in the Salem version are printed below under notes *d and *g.

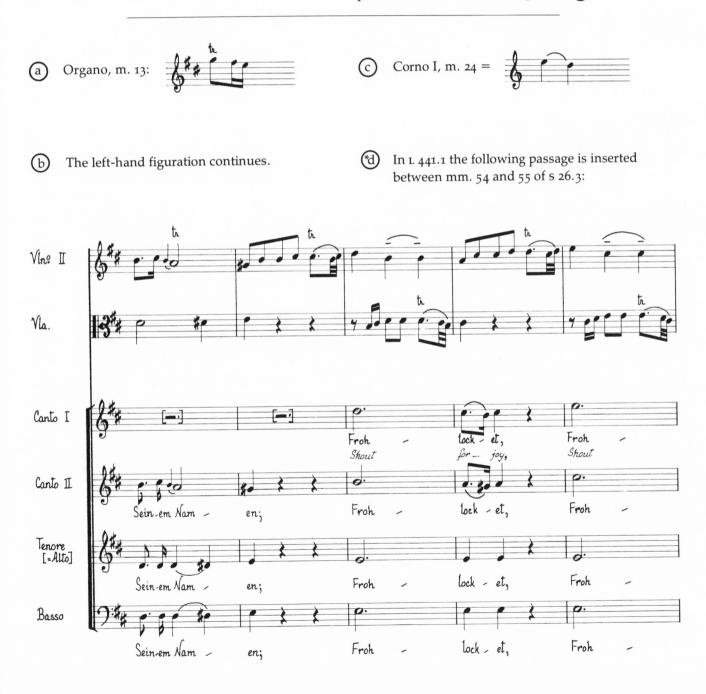

ⓐ Organo, m. 13:

ⓑ The left-hand figuration continues.

ⓒ Corno I, m. 24 =

*d In L 441.1 the following passage is inserted between mm. 54 and 55 of s 26.3:

lock - et, ihr stark - en Held - en, die ihr Sein - en Be-fehl aus-richt - et;
for joy, ye might - y her - oes, those who fol - low the Lord's com-mand-ments;

(e) s 26.3: Flute I (m. 58) omits the accidental before the appoggiatura; s 26.3: Canto I (m. 58) contains an obvious scribal error:

L 441.1: Canto I omits the appoggiatura.

The best reading of this passage for Flutes I and II, Violin I, Canto I is:

(f) s 26.3: Flute I (m. 74) contains an obvious error:

(g) For mm. 76–79 in the Salem manuscript, the Lititz version substitutes this passage (see the following page):

 In the manuscript, Corno II (m. 83) reads:

 Organo, m. 91 =

 Flute I, Violin I, m. 91 =
Flute II, Violin II, m. 91 =

 The Canto Basso part (m. 102) contains an obvious error:

In the same measure:
Violin I, Canto I, Organo =
Violin II =
Canto Alto =

Canto Basso, Basso =

[*IV. Chorale*]

Sources

Text. / Source unknown; ALF, trans.

Tune. / GC Art 230.[25]

Harmonization. / SB no. 136. Parts: soprano, alto, tenor, bass.

[*V.*] Recitativ.

Also performed at the peace festival held in Gnadenfrey on 13 March 1763.

Sources

Text. / II.Moses 15:3; Psalms 46:10; 74:20; 12:5,6; MPG, trans. The complete text is given in the description of the Gnadenfrey peace festival.[26]

Musical Setting. / Unidentified.

Music Manuscripts.

L 441.2.[27] Parts: Canto Basso. The only surviving part for this composition has been transcribed faithfully. The extant string parts, Violino Secondo and Viola, as well as the other vocal parts in the manuscript are marked "*Tacet*," so it can be assumed that the recitative was accompanied only by continuo.

[*VI. Chorale*]

Sources

Text. / Source unknown; MPG, trans.

Tune. / GC 119.[28]

Harmonization. / SB no. 72. Parts: soprano, alto, tenor, bass.

[*VII.*] Duetto.

Also performed at the peace festival held in Gnadenfrey on 13 March 1763.

Sources

Text. / Psalm 147:14; MPG, trans. The complete text is given in the description of the Gnadenfrey peace festival.[29]

Musical Setting. / Unidentified.

Music Manuscripts.

L 441.3.[30] Parts: Canto Primo, Canto Secondo; Violino Secondo, Viola.

This edition contains a transcription of the extant parts listed above.

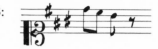 Canto Primo, m. 18:

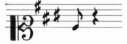 Canto Secondo, m. 28:

[*VIII. Chorale*]

Sources

Text. / Source unknown; MPG, trans.

Tune. / GC 214A.[31]

Harmonization. / SB no. 126. Parts: soprano, alto, tenor, bass.

[*IX.*] Recitativ.

Also performed at the peace festival held in Gnadenfrey on 13 March 1763.

Sources

Text. / Unidentified; MPG, trans. The complete text is given in the description of the Gnadenfrey peace festival.[32]

Musical Setting. / Unidentified.

Music Manuscripts.

L 441.8.[33] Parts: Canto Basso. The Salem *Freudenpsalm* utilizes only the opening recitative section of a more extended composition. The extant string parts, Violino Secondo and Viola, as well as the other vocal parts are marked "*Tacet*," so it can be assumed that the recitative was accompanied only by continuo.

[*X. Chorale-Anthem*] Arietta.

Sources

Text. / Source unknown; ALF, trans.

Musical Setting. / A chorale prelude for organ, "Herzlich thut mich verlangen," by J. P. Kellner,[34] adapted by Christian Gregor (1763).[35] GC Art 151A is the basis of the setting.

Music Manuscripts.

1. s 196.2[36] (old No. 63).[37] Parts: Canto Primo, Canto Secondo; Flauto; Violoncello ô Fagotto; Violino Primo, Violino Secondo, Viola, Basso; Organo.

This manuscript contains a setting of the text "Ach Schönster unter allen."[38] The obbligato parts for flute and violoncello or bassoon are derived from Gregor's first version of this adaptation, setting the text "Siehe, du hast Lust zur Wahrheit";[39] these parts appear to be later additions to the manuscript since they are not mentioned in any of the 1808 catalogs of the collection and they were prepared by a different copyist.

2. ss 80.[40] Parts: Canto Primo, Canto Secondo. The Canto Primo part is marked "di Gregor."

3. h 26.1. Score.

The music in this edition is based on s 196.2; the original text has been replaced by the poem contained in the *Freudenpsalm*. The parts for flute and violoncello or bassoon are presented on smaller staves to indicate the probability that they were not used in the 1783 Fourth of July performance.

(a) s 196.2, Organo, m. 12:

(b) s 196.2, Violin I, m. 13:

(c) s 196.2, Basso, m. 38:

[XI. Chorale]

Sources

Text. / Source unknown; MPG, trans.

Tune. / GC 230.[41]

Harmonization. / SB no. 136. Parts: soprano, alto, tenor, bass.

[XII. Chorale]

Sources

Text. / Source unknown; MPG, trans.

Tune. / GC 37A.[42]

[XIII. Chorale]

Sources

Text. / Source unknown; ALF, trans.

Tune. / GC 169.[43]

Harmonization. / SB no. 111. Parts: soprano, alto, tenor, bass.

[XIV. Chorale]

Also performed at the peace festival in Herrnhut on 21 March 1763 during the afternoon Lovefeast.

Sources

Text. / Source unknown; MPG, trans. In the description of the Herrnhut peace festival, the text begins "*Du gibst* Fried in *unserm* Lande."[44]

Tune. / GC 23, first two phrases only.[45]

Harmonization. / SB no. 23. Parts: soprano, alto, tenor, bass. The partbooks contain only the first two phrases of the chorale.

[XV. Anthem]

Also performed at the peace festival held in Herrnhut on 21 March 1763 as the eleventh anthem in the *Danck- und Freudenpsalm* presented during the afternoon (2 P.M.) Lovefeast.[46]

Sources

Text. / Psalms 85:10–13; 145:16; MPG, trans. The complete text is given in the description of the Herrnhut peace festival.

Musical Setting. / Christian Gregor (1763).

Music Manuscripts.

　　1. s 154.10 (old No. 69).[47] Parts: Canto Primo, Canto Secondo, Alto, Canto Basso; Violino Primo, Violino Secondo, Viola, Basso; Organo.

　　2. ss 2.2. Parts: Canto Primo, Canto Secondo, Alto.

　　3. H 22.11. Score.

Because of its completeness, s 154.10 has been used as the principal source for this edition. Since the instrumental parts in that manuscript are apparently of post-1783 origin and are transposed a whole step higher than the original key as it appears in the 1763 Herbst score and in the vocal parts, they have been checked carefully against the Herbst score and have been returned to their original key.

(a)　See the paragraph above.

(b)　s 154.10 and ss 2.2, Alto, m. 3:　

(c)　Violin I, Violin II, Viola, m. 18 =　

(d)　All the vocal parts contain the tempo mark *"Munter"*; the comparative form of the same adjective, *"Munterer,"* appears on the Organo part, while its contracted version, *"Muntrer,"* is found on all the string parts.

(e)　s 154.10 and ss 2.2, Canto 2, m. 29:　

(f)　s 154.10, Violin II, m. 31 (transposed to original key):

The Herbst score gives this version of m. 31:

(g)　Canto Basso, m. 31 =　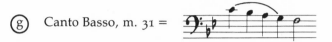

in agreement with the Basso and Organo parts. See "Das ist ein Tag," prepared by the same copyist (*Freudenpsalm* II, m. 7, note (a)).

[*Chorale-Response*]

Also performed following the anthem "Dass in unserm Lande" at the peace festival held in Herrnhut on 21 March 1763.[48]

Sources

Text. / Source unknown; MPG, trans.

Tune. / GC 4 (ending).

　　Harmonization. / SB no. 2. Parts: soprano, alto, tenor, bass.

[*XVI. Anthem*]

Sources

Text. / Psalms 147:12; 148:12, 13; 149:1,3; 150:2–6; MPG, trans.

Musical Setting. / C. L. Brau or J. C. Geisler.[49]

Music Manuscripts.

　　1. s 26.1 (old No. 101). Parts: Canto Primo, Canto Secondo, Canto Alto, Canto Basso; Corno Primo, Corno Secondo; Flauto Traverso Primo, Flauto Traverso Secondo; Violino Primo, Violino Secondo, Viola, Basso; Organo.

　　2. ss 5.1. Parts: Canto Primo, Canto Secondo, Canto Alto, Canto Basso.

　　3. H 117.3. Score.

This edition is based on the complete set of parts contained in s 26.1.

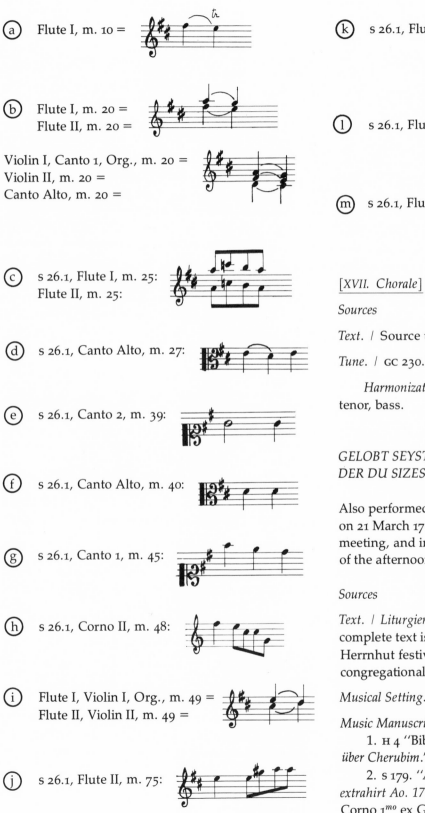

(a) Flute I, m. 10 =

(b) Flute I, m. 20 =
Flute II, m. 20 =

Violin I, Canto 1, Org., m. 20 =
Violin II, m. 20 =
Canto Alto, m. 20 =

(c) s 26.1, Flute I, m. 25:
Flute II, m. 25:

(d) s 26.1, Canto Alto, m. 27:

(e) s 26.1, Canto 2, m. 39:

(f) s 26.1, Canto Alto, m. 40:

(g) s 26.1, Canto 1, m. 45:

(h) s 26.1, Corno II, m. 48:

(i) Flute I, Violin I, Org., m. 49 =
Flute II, Violin II, m. 49 =

(j) s 26.1, Flute II, m. 75:

(k) s 26.1, Flute I, m. 76:

(l) s 26.1, Flute II, m. 85:

(m) s 26.1, Flute II, m. 101:

[*XVII. Chorale*]

Sources

Text. / Source unknown; MPG, trans.

Tune. / GC 230.[50]

Harmonization. / SB no. 136. Parts: soprano, alto, tenor, bass.

GELOBT SEYST DU,
DER DU SIZEST ÜBER CHERUBIM

Also performed at the peace festivals in Herrnhut on 21 March 1763, at the beginning of the 8 A.M. meeting, and in Barby on the same day, at the end of the afternoon Lovefeast.

Sources

Text. / *Liturgien-Buchlein, I.*; MPG, trans. The complete text is also given in the account of the Herrnhut festival,[51] in which the passages requiring congregational participation are labeled "*Gem.*"

Musical Setting. / Christian Gregor (1759).

Music Manuscripts.
   1. H 4 "Bibel-Gesang: *Gelobt seyst du der du sizest über Cherubim.*" Score.
   2. S 179. "*Aus der alten Composition von 1759 extrahirt Ao. 1791.*" Parts: Canto 1mo, Canto 2do, Basso; Corno 1mo ex G dur, Corno 2do ex G dur; Violino 1mo,

Violino 2do, Viola, Basso; Organo. Each part bears the citation: *"Bibel Gesang / s. Lit. Buchl. No. 1."*

    3. ss 19.1. Parts: Canto 1mo, Canto 2do, Basso.

Since the Salem manuscripts (s 179 and ss 19.1) are based on the revised Moravian liturgies published in 1791—eight years after the Fourth of July festival—they have been of limited value in the preparation of this edition. The 1791 revision contains numerous changes in musical content and deletions of significant portions of the original composition. This three-voiced version does not provide four-part harmonizations for the congregational responses and several of the original formulae are altered or omitted. Deletions include mm. 57–66, 92–97, 107–17, as well as the sections that refer to warfare ("Mitten wir im Kriege hat Er uns behalten" and the final chorale quotation: "Und so kriegt Jesus Jehovah . . . "). The initial line of text is also changed to read: "Gelobet seyst du, der du thronest über Cherubim."

It is understandable that copies of the original composition, which may have been a part of the Salem Collections at one time, have not survived, for these libraries were intended to provide music for performance; superceded liturgies, having no practical use, would be discarded. Fortunately, the Herbst Collection of scores is a reference library in which the older version of this composition has been preserved. This edition, therefore, is based primarily on the Herbst manuscript score (H 4), with the addition of some details found in the Salem manuscripts that may provide clues to the performance practices of the Salem musicians.

Herbst rarely labeled parts on his scores, so the attributions given in this edition include those found on the corresponding Salem parts (enclosed in parentheses) and editorial additions (in brackets) that are based on the clefs used and the position of the parts within the score. Herbst also omits the skeletal organ parts that are always present in the practical collections; therefore, the passage reproduced here is transcribed from the organ part for the revised version found in Salem (s 179). Some performance instructions in the Herbst score that are missing on the Salem parts are circled in this edition to indicate

the possibility that Salem musicians may not have followed those instructions when performing even the early version of this composition. Particularly noticeable in the Salem vocal parts is the absence of all the vocal trills that are indicated in the Herbst manuscript.

In attempting to retain the flavor of Herbst's score, this edition follows as many of his copying methods as possible, e.g., the placement of the horn parts on separate staves, the numbering of each measure of rests, and the use of time-saving shorthand methods (see notes (b) and (g) below). Here, as in many of his scores, Herbst has ignored the common practice of capitalizing words referring to the Deity. This edition follows Herbst's version, but it should be noted that the Salem manuscripts as well as the complete text given in the account of the Herrnhut peace festival observe the traditional capitalization or double capitalization of such words as Du, GOtt, HErr, and JEsu. The Herrnhut account contains information concerning the performance of this composition that does not appear in the Herbst score, in particular, the use of congregational singing accompanied by brass instruments; this information has been included in the present edition (see notes (c), (e), and (h) below).

(a)   The beginning of the organ part accompanying the revised version of this composition (s 179) has been given here as a guide to the actual sound of the 1783 Fourth of July performance. The remainder of the part, of course, cannot be used in conjunction with the original composition because it follows the 1791 revision of the work.

(b)

indicates that this part doubles the part immediately above.

(c)   In the Herrnhut account, the text is interrupted at this point and the following description is inserted: "Die ganze Gemeine wiederholte unter dem Trompeten- und Posaunen-Schall diese Worte: *Ihn ewiglich*" ("The entire congregation under the pealing trumpets and trombones repeated these words: *Ihn ewiglich*"). In the Herbst manuscript, the four-part harmonizations in an otherwise three-voice choral texture are no doubt intended for performance by the brasses mentioned in the account. The remainder of the congregational responses are labeled "*Gem.*" in the Herrnhut account and the text is not underlined. In this edition, the responses for congregation and brasses are labeled "*Gem.*", the text is underlined, and brackets are inserted to delineate the passages.

(d) Canto I, m. 34 =
Alto, m. 34 =

(e) *Text.* | GG 331, stanza 4.[52]

Tune. | GrC 132g.[53]

The congregation and brasses join in this chorale quotation.

(f) In the Herbst score, a new set of numbers begins after the chorale section.

(g) The instrumental bass doubles the vocal bass part, which, in the Herbst score, is written on the staff immediately above the instrumental bass.

(h) *Text.* | GG 1044, stanza 9.

Tune. | GC 15.

As in the previous chorale section, the congregation and brasses join the chorus and orchestra in performing the chorale.

(i) The Herrnhut account gives the following text for the remainder of the composition: "ein fröliches Hallelujah zu Seines Namens Ehre."

NOTES

CHAPTER 1

1. Other Moravian settlements having a connection with this study are Barby, Gnadenberg, Gnadenfrey, and Niesky in Europe and, in America, Bethlehem, Lititz, and Nazareth in Pennsylvania and Bethabara and Salem in North Carolina.

2. Although it has no direct bearing on this study, it should be mentioned that the traditional Easter Sunrise Service originated in Herrnhut in 1732 when a group of young men, following the example of the Disciples, gathered at the burial ground at dawn on Easter Sunday. What was an impromptu service has become one of the most impressive events in the Moravian Church year, highlighted by the antiphonal performance of chorales by the church bands stationed at several separate locations in the graveyard.

3. August Gottlieb Spangenberg, *Kurzgefasste historische Nachricht von der gegenwärtigen Verfassung der evangelischen Brüderunität augspurgischer Confession* (Frankfurt, 1774).

4. Traugott Bagge, trans. A Short Historical Account about the Present Constitution of the Protestant Unity of Brethren of the Augustan Confession. Translated from the German Edition, Printed at Francfort and Leipzig [in] 1774 (1778). A manuscript copy of Bagge's translation of Spangenberg's *Kurzgefasste historische Nachricht* is preserved in the Moravian Archives in Winston-Salem, N.C. On the inside of the front cover, a signature of ownership "Alexʳ Martin" shows that this copy was once the property of the governor of North Carolina serving at the time of the 4 July 1783 observance. After Martin's signature, the letters "LLD" have been added in a different hand. Also on the inner cover, and in still another hand, is the notation "this Manuscript was found in his Library after his decease. J. A. Martin. March 1808." Bagge's translation, with a few passages omitted, is reprinted in Adelaide L. Fries et al., *Records of the Moravians in North Carolina* (Raleigh, N.C.: State Department of Archives and History, 1922–), 3:977–1018 (hereafter cited as *Records*).

5. Bagge, Account of the Unity of Brethren, sec. 3, art. 18. The original German (Spangenberg, *Kurzgefasste historische Nachricht*, p. 73), reads: "Der Gesang in den Brüderversamlungen hat etwas sehr liebliches, weil er sich von dem sonst gewöhnlichen lauten Schreyen der Lieder sehr entfernet und desto andächtiger und harmonischer wird. Die Lieder, welche dermalen im Gebrauche sind, stehen meist in dem kleinen Brüdergesangbuche und sind theils aus den alten Kernliedern der Brüderunität und evangelischlutherischen Kirche, theils aus Paul Gerhards und anderer neuer Liederdichter Samlungen herausgenommen. Die vor einem Viertelseculo einmal in der Gemeine aufgekommenen Gesänge, die zwar gewiss den ihnen theils aus Spott, theils aus Misverstand angedichteten Sinn nicht gehabt, gleichwol auch der Einfalt und Ernsthaftigkeit der göttlichen Wahrheit zum Theil nicht angemessen und mit allerley Wortspielen, die ins tändelhafte fallen, vermengt waren, sind längst aus allem Gebrauche gesetzt.

"Ja die Lehrer in der Brüderkirche haben sich alle Mühe gegeben, sich auch in Liedern, von Zeit zu Zeit, verständlicher, lauterer und einfältiger auszudrükken und so zu fassen, dass ein andächtig nachdenkendes Herz, bey dem Gebrauche derselben, über die Frage: Verstehst du auch, was du singest? nicht Anstand nehmen, oder gar schweigen dürfe."

6. Bagge, Account of the Unity of Brethren, sec. 3, art. 15. Spangenberg, *Kurzgefasste historische Nachricht*, p. 70, reads: "Gegen fünf Uhr ist eine liturgische Versamlung der Abendmahlsgenossen, darinnen ein feyerlicher Gesang zum Vater, Sohn und heiligen Geist gemeinschaftlich abgesungen wird."

7. The congregation was seated by Choirs, with the women placed to the minister's right and the men to his left.

8. Bagge, Account of the Unity of Brethren, sec. 3, art. 16. Spangenberg, *Kurzgefasste historische Nachricht*, pp. 71–72, reads: "Ausser der vorgedachten liturgischen Versamlung am Sonntage, werden auch in den Wochentagen, einige Versamlungen zur Absingung dergleichen Lob- und Dankgesänge angewendet, darunter zeichnet sich besonders der Gesang: *O Haupt voll Blut und Wunden*, Freytags Abends aus. Auch wird in diesen liturgischen Versamlungen der Friedenskuss von einem jeglichen an den neben ihm stehenden sowol auf der Brüder als auf der Schwestern Seite, ertheilt, und zwar bey solchen Worten des Gesangs, die auf den Liebes- und Friedensbund der Gemein unter einander, einen Bezug haben.

"Es wechseln auch in diesen liturgischen Gesängen die Brüder und Schwestern ab, so dass einige Zeilen von jenen, wiederum einige von diesen, und wieder andere von beiden zugleich gesungen werden: wodurch der Gesang lieblicher und die Gegenwärtigkeit des Gemüthes befördert wird."

9. Christian Gregor, ed. *Choral-buch, enthaltend alle zu dem Gesangbuche der evangelischen Brüder-Gemeinen vom Jahre 1778 gehörige Melodien* (Leipzig, 1784). In items 5 and 6 of his instructions on the use of the choralebook, Gregor explains the antiphonal method of singing chorales and cites specific examples in detail.

10. Autograph copy in Archiv der Brüder-Unität, Herrnhut, East Germany; microfilm copy in the Moravian Music Foundation, Winston-Salem, N.C. A printed memoir, differing in a few details, appears in *Nachrichten aus der Brüder-Gemeine*, Gnadau, 64. Jahrgang, Oktober, 1882, I., 865–903, and *Beiträge zur Erbauung aus der Brüder-Gemeine*, C. F. Stückelberger, ed., Gnadau, 2. Jahrgang, I., 427–78. Copies of the *Nachrichten* and *Beiträge* are housed in the Archives of the Moravian Church, Winston-Salem, N.C. English translations of both memoirs are given in Jane Stuart Smith, "Christian Gregor: A Critical Edition of His Autobiography and a Contribution to the Study of Autobiographical Writings of the 18th Century Pietists" (Ph.D. diss., University of North Carolina, 1962).

11. Manuscript copies of a large number of Gregor's works are preserved in the various music collections in the custody of the Moravian Music Foundation.

12. Only the texts of the Psalms were printed. The musical settings are in manuscript form.

13. Bagge, Account of the Unity of Brethren, sec. 3, art. 18. Spangenberg, *Kurzgefasste historische Nachricht*, p. 74, reads: " Zu den Festen der ganzen christlichen Kirche sowol, als den der Brüderkirche eigenen feyerlichen Gedenktagen, sind auch von Zeit zu Zeit einige Psalmen oder Cantaten gefertiget und gedrukt worden. Diese werden von dem *Choro musico* einer jeden Gemeine, mit einer sanften Instrumentalmusic abgesungen, und von der Gemeine, mit darunter gemengten zur Materie passenden Choralen begleitet."

14. Musical scores of complete Psalms compiled by Gregor, Geisler, and Herbst are preserved in the Johannes Herbst Collection housed in the Moravian Music Foundation. See Marilyn Gombosi, ed., *Catalog of the Johannes Herbst Collection* (Chapel Hill, N.C.: University of North Carolina Press, 1970).

15. Bagge, Account of the Unity of Brethren, sec. 3, art. 12. Spangenberg, *Kurzgefasste historische Nachricht*, p. 67, reads:"Um neun Uhr des Abends und also kurz vor dem Schlafengehen, ist noch eine allgemeine Versamlung, darinnen gemeiniglich die

Materie derjenigen Sprüche, die an dem Tage zum Grunde der
Erbauung gelegt worden, mit allerley dieselbe erläuternden Versen
besungen wird. Und das heist eine Singstunde."

CHAPTER 2

1. Born in 1704 in Prussia, Spangenberg was educated at the
University of Jena, receiving a Master of Arts degree, and was
ordained a Lutheran minister. In 1732 he moved to the University
of Halle to teach in the theological school and help direct the
orphanage. Dismissed from his post because of his friendship with
Count Zinzendorf, Spangenberg joined the Moravians in Herrnhut
where his organizational talents were soon recognized and
appreciated. Spangenberg led the first Moravian mission to
Savannah, Georgia, in 1735 and subsequently visited Pennsylvania
to assess the condition of the German settlers in that region and to
gather information concerning the Indians among whom the
Moravians intended to carry on mission work. Recalled to Europe,
Spangenberg was named treasurer of the Unity and was placed in
charge of all Unity affairs while Zinzendorf visited America. In
1744, Spangenberg was consecrated a bishop and chosen to head
the Unity in America; he was charged with the responsibility of
organizing the American Moravian settlements and carrying on the
Indian missions. After Zinzendorf's death in 1760, Spangenberg
returned to Europe to help direct the affairs of the Unity. During
his tenure, the constitution of the Unity was drafted, the economic
affairs of the society were placed on a sound basis, synods were
formed, schools were established, and the musical practices of the
Moravian Church described in chapter 1 were crystallized.
Spangenberg's keen interest in education and music is manifested
in a number of his books, including the *Kurzgefasste historische
Nachricht* (1774), quoted at length in the notes to chapter 1, and in
his hymnbook for children, *Gesangbuchlein für die Kinder in den
Brüdergemeinen* (Barby, 1789). "Brother Joseph," as he was known
affectionately, died in 1792.

2. *Records*, 1:59.

3. The men selected for the assignment were chosen for their
particular trades and talents which were needed in the pioneering
venture; among them were cooks, gardeners, a surgeon, a
shoemaker, a millwright, a carpenter, a farmer, a shepherd, a tailor,
and one of the original surveyors. Most of them were residents of
Christiansspring, a farming community lying just outside
Nazareth, Pennsylvania, which had been named in honor of Count
Zinzendorf's son, Christian Renatus. See *Records*, 1:73, 74.

4. Travel Diary, Sunday, 7 Oct. 1753, *Records*, 1:75.

5. *Records*, 1:79. The translation given here is by Adelaide L. Fries,
the late archivist of the Moravian Church in America, Southern
Province; Miss Fries's translation preserves the original meter of
the verse, 86 86 86 86 (Common Meter). There are a number of
tunes in the Moravian chorale repertoire that can accommodate
Common Meter, so that it is impossible to determine the specific
tune sung by the colonists during this first Lovefeast in North
Carolina.

6. Bethabara Diary, Monday, 19 Nov. 1753, *Records*, 1:80.

7. Bethabara Diary, Sabbath (Saturday), 23 Feb. 1754, *Records*, 1:96.

8. Bethabara Diary, 22 July 1755, and Travel Diary of the Little
Pilgrim Congregation, Tuesday, 4 Nov. 1755, *Records*, 1:134, 146.

9. Bethabara Diary, Wednesday, 1 Jan. 1755, *Records*, 1:122.

10. Wachovia Diary, Saturday, 15 Nov. 1755, *Records*, 1:148.

11. Bethabara Diary, 26 Aug. 1756, *Records*, 1:172.

12. Bethabara Diary, 24 Dec. 1756, *Records*, 1:174.

13. A *Saal* was a hall used for congregation meetings and worship
services when a church edifice was not available.

14. Wachovia Diary, 8 July 1762, *Records*, 1:247.

15. The *Gemein Haus*, or *Gemeinhaus*, was the Congregation House
containing the *Saal* as well as living quarters for leaders of the
congregation.

16. Manuscript preserved in the Moravian Archives, Winston-
Salem, N.C.

17. *Records*, 1:260. Entry for 16 May 1762 in the Travel Diary kept by
the colonists who delivered the organ to Bethabara (see p. 8).

18. *Aufseher Collegium* Minutes, Tuesday, 15 Jan. 1782, Erika Huber,
trans., Moravian Archives, Winston-Salem, N.C. Bonn had arrived
in Wachovia in 1766 to serve as physician and surgeon.

19. Wachovia Memorabilia for 1768, *Records*, 1:369.

20. Translated in its entirety in *Records*, 1:353–55.

21. Bethabara Diary, 5 June 1771, *Records*, 1:463.

22. Bethabara Diary, 6 June 1771, ibid.

23. Bethabara Diary, 6 June 1771, *Records*, 1:465.

24. Bethabara became known as "Old Town," an appellation that is
still in use.

25. *Helfer Conferenz* Minutes, 14 Feb. 1765, *Records*, 1:310.

26. Bethabara Diary, 6 Jan. 1766, *Records*, 1:323.

27. The cornerstone of the *Gemeinhaus* was laid on 17 April 1770
and work continued on the exterior of the building throughout the
summer. With the placement of the roof timbers, completed on 18
September, the trombonists climbed to the top of the building and,
perched on the roof, played several chorales to mark the occasion
(Wachovia Diary, 17 April 1770, *Records*, 1:404–7).

28. Salem Diary, 13 Nov. 1771, *Records*, 1:444–47.

29. *Aeltesten Conferenz* Minutes, 20 June 1769, Edmund Schwarze,
trans., Moravian Archives, Winston-Salem, N.C.

30. *Aeltesten Conferenz* Minutes, 18 Dec. 1770, ibid.

31. The spelling of this name gave the Moravians considerable
difficulty; the records contain such variants as Bulitschek,
Bultischek, and Bolejak.

32. Bullitschek made the cabinet used for storing the Bethabara
archives. See *Records*, 2:729.

33. Bethabara Diary, 22 Jan. 1773, *Records*, 2:777.

34. In a letter to the Unity Elders Conference concerning the
rebuilding of the Salem flour mill (1775), J. M. Graff describes
Bullitschek as "the only capable mill-wright in the
neighborhood . . . he charges a good deal and is slow" (*Records*,
2:884).

35. *Aeltesten Conferenz* Minutes, 30 Dec. 1771, Edmund Schwarze,
trans.

36. *Aeltesten Conferenz* Minutes, 21 Jan. 1772, ibid.

37. The small organ brought by J. M. Graff from Bethlehem in
1762. See p. 8.

38. *Aeltesten Conferenz* Minutes, 4 Feb. 1772, Edmund Schwarze,
trans.

39. *Helfer Conferenz* Minutes, 4 May 1772, *Records*, 2:723.

40. Salem Diary, 6 and 7 Oct. 1772, *Records*, 2:690.

41. Ibid. A manuscript copy of Marshall's report, filed in the
Moravian Archives, Winston-Salem, N.C., shows that Marshall
began his report on 29 August 1772 and continued to add to it for
several months. On the manuscript, the dates and months are

marked off one by one: "29 Aug., Sept., Oct."; the report was finally completed in November 1772.

42. The Salem Bullitschek organ was removed from the *Gemeinsaal* in 1798 to make room for the new Tannenberg organ. It was taken to the Single Brothers' *Saal* in Bethabara and disappeared in the nineteenth century. A twin instrument built in 1773 (Figure B) by Bullitschek for the Bethania *Saal* survived until 1942, when it was destroyed by fire. Much present knowledge of the Salem organ is, in fact, based on the Bethania instrument.

43. Memorabilia for 1772, *Records*, 2:661.

44. Filed with Congregation Council Minutes for 1774, Erika Huber, trans., Moravian Archives, Winston-Salem, N.C.

45. Paul Tiersch was the first preacher in Salem, a post he held until his death on 16 October 1774 (*Records*, 2:819). Among his other duties, Tiersch helped with the direction of the music for the Salem Congregation and served as archivist; upon his death, Johann Michael Graff, who had moved to Salem from Bethabara, was chosen to take charge of the congregation music, keep the archives, and lead services (*Records*, 2:829).

46. Salem Diary, 24 Jan. 1772, *Records*, 2:668.

47. Ibid., p. 671. The translation given in the *Records* differs from the original manuscript in its substitution of the term *Vorsteher* for *Diener*, as given in the original.

48. *Aufseher Collegium* Minutes, 28 Sept. 1772, *Records*, 2:705.

49. *Die Gemein-Casse in Salem*, 1773–74, 1776–77, 1778–79, Moravian Archives, Winston-Salem, N.C.

50. *Helfer Conferenz* Minutes, 20 Sept. 1773, Edmund Schwarze, trans.: "Whatever Br. Bonn collects in voluntary gifts among the Married People and the Single Brethren for a musicians' treasure (for strings) Br. Praezel will receive and carry an account." Entries for 18 July 1774 in the Single Brothers' account list: *"für die Orgel des gleichen* [the *Saal*] 5/15/4" and *"für music an Gottesacker* [the Moravian graveyard, "God's Acre"] -/15/-" (Moravian Archives,Winston-Salem, N.C.). Filed with this manuscript is a 1790 subscription list for the 1798 Tannenberg organ.

51. *Helfer Conferenz* Minutes, 4 Aug. 1777, Edmund Schwarze, trans.

52. *Aufseher Collegium* Minutes, 20 Aug. 1777, Erika Huber, trans.

53. *Helfer Conferenz* Minutes, 18 May 1772.

54. *Helfer Conferenz* Minutes, 30 Oct. 1775, Edmund Schwarze, trans.

55. Letter to Traugott Bagge, dated 26 Aug. 1777. Reprinted in its entirety in *Records*, 3:1365–66.

56. *Records*, 3:1366.

57. *Aufseher Collegium* Minutes, 1 Dec. 1772, Erika Huber, trans.

58. *Aufseher Collegium* Minutes, 15 Dec. 1779, *Records*, 3:1329.

59. The boys were separated into two age groups, each of which had its own schoolroom.

60. *Aeltesten Conferenz* Minutes, 8 Jan. 1780, *Records*, 4:1581.

61. *Aeltesten Conferenz* Minutes, 27 Sept. 1780, *Records*, 4:1603.

62. *Helfer Conferenz* Minutes, 4 April 1782, *Records*, 4:1803.

63. *Aeltesten Conferenz* Minutes, 12 Sept. 1781, *Records*, 4:1729.

64. Peter's *Lebenslauf* (autobiography) is preserved in the Moravian Archives, Bethlehem, Pa. Born in Heerendijk, Holland, in 1746, Friedrich Peter was educated in Moravian schools in Germany and then emigrated to America in 1770. After working for a decade with the Moravians in Pennsylvania (1770–73: Nazareth; 1773–79: Bethlehem; 1779–80: Lititz), Peter was transferred to Salem, North Carolina, bringing with him his manuscript copies of European instrumental music that he had made during his student days at the Moravian seminary in Barby; these copies form the core of an extensive library of secular instrumental music now in the custody of the Moravian Music Foundation, Winston-Salem, N.C. During his tenure as music director in Salem, Peter composed a set of six string quintets, believed to be the earliest chamber music composed in America. Preserved in holograph score and parts, filed in the Moravian Archives in Bethlehem, Pa., the quintets were edited by Hans T. David and published for the New York Public Library by C. F. Peters Corporation in 1955. In addition to his work with the instrumentalists in each Moravian community he served, Peter also filled the post of organist and composed quantities of sacred music, including solo songs as well as anthems with orchestral accompaniment. Manuscript copies of his sacred works are preserved in the Moravian Archives in Bethlehem, Pa., and in the headquarters of the Moravian Music Foundation, Winston-Salem, N.C.

65. Letter dated September 1780 from F. W. Marshall to Joachim Heinrich Andresen, a member of the Unity Elders Conference (*Records*, 4:1896–1904).

66. *Aeltesten Conferenz* Minutes, 17 June 1780, Edmund Schwarze, trans.

67. *Aufseher Collegium* Minutes, 27 June 1780, *Records*, 4:1591. The Diacony had also paid Peter's moving expenses; see its financial records, folio 78: "An Reise und fracht für Fried. Peter von Bethlehem. 23/-8"(Moravian Archives, Winston-Salem, N.C.).

68. *Aeltesten Conferenz* Minutes, 13 Sept. 1780.

69. Congregation Council Minutes, 14 Dec. 1780.

70. *Aeltesten Conferenz* Minutes, 16 Sept. 1780.

71. Salem Diary, 5 Nov. 1780, *Records*, 4:1575.

72. Salem Diary, 30 Dec. 1780, *Records*, 4:1580.

73. *Aeltesten Conferenz* Minutes, 20 Dec. 1780, *Records*, 4:1612.

74. *Aeltesten Conferenz* Minutes, 4 Dec. 1782, *Records*, 4:1809.

75. Salem Diary, 17 May 1785, *Records*, 5:2082.

76. *Aeltesten Conferenz* Minutes, 11 Dec. 1782.

77. *Aeltesten Conferenz* Minutes, 11 Nov. 1784. The minutes show that the Elders were seriously concerned with the propriety of naming an unmarried man as preacher of the Salem Congregation. During the meeting—the only such meeting held during this period that Peter did not attend and take the minutes of—five prospective brides for Peter were proposed and all were rejected by the Lot; the Elders finally concluded that it was the Saviour's will that Peter remain a bachelor for the time being. It was not until 1786 that Peter married Catharina Leinbach. For explanation of the Moravians' use of the Lot, see *Records*, 2:555–56, and William K. Hoyt, "The Lot, the Youth and the Schobers," in *The Three Forks of Muddy Creek*, ed. Frances Griffin (Winston-Salem, N.C.: Old Salem, Inc., 1974–), 1:43–53.

78. Congregation Council Minutes, 5 Dec. 1782.

79. *Aufseher Collegium* Minutes, 5 Dec. 1782.

80. *Aeltesten Conferenz* Minutes, 14 Dec. 1782.

81. Salem Diary, 23 Aug. 1790, *Records*, 5:2300.

82. *Aeltesten Conferenz* Minutes, 30 June 1790, *Records*, 5:2307.

83. *Aeltesten Conferenz* Minutes, 3 July 1790, ibid.

84. *Aufseher Collegium* Minutes, 6 July 1790, Erika Huber, trans.

85. *Aeltesten Conferenz* Minutes, 7 July 1790, *Records*, 5:2308.

86. *Aeltesten Conferenz* Minutes, 7 July 1790, ibid.

87. *Helfer Conferenz* Minutes, 19 Aug. 1790, ibid.

88. *Aufseher Collegium* Minutes, 4 July 1780.

89. Ibid., 9 Aug. 1780.

90. Ibid., 28 Nov. 1780, Erika Huber, trans.

91. *Musicalische Cassa*, entry for 28 Dec. 1780, in *Cassa-Buch der Musikalischen Collecte seit 1780*, Moravian Music Foundation, Winston-Salem, N.C. The music accounts were kept in small unbound booklets, several of which are preserved in the archives of the Moravian Music Foundation, Winston-Salem, N.C. The accounts kept by Friedrich Peter (1780–82) are models of clarity and neatness; his successor, Johannes Reuz, was not as meticulous in his record-keeping.

92. *Musicalische Cassa*, entries for 29 Dec. 1780 and 8 Feb. 1781, in *Cassa-Buch der Musikalischen Collecte seit 1780*.

93. Such discussions concerning the Bullitschek organ were to continue for seventeen years, until the Moravians finally were able to purchase an organ from David Tannenberg. The 1798 Tannenberg organ has been restored and placed in the *Saal* of the Brothers' House in Old Salem. A second, larger Tannenberg instrument that stood in the Salem Home Moravian Church for many years before its dismantlement awaits restoration.

94. The open back of the organ case, which faced into the *Saal*, allowed the full sound of the unenclosed pipes and mechanism to reach the congregation.

95. *Helfer Conferenz* Minutes, 19 April 1781, *Records*, 4:1719.

96. Salem Diary, 31 May 1781, *Records*, 4:1694.

97. *Helfer Conferenz* Minutes, 9 July 1781.

98. Wachovia Memorabilia for 1781, *Records*, 4:1661.

99. Salem Diary, 17 July 1781, *Records*, 4:1697.

100. The Salem records for the war years contain countless references to indignities and frightening incidents suffered by the Moravians in Wachovia. The move to deprive them of their land was based on the fact that they had purchased the tract from Lord Granville, an Englishman. An official account of the war and its effect upon the Wachovia settlements was prepared by Friedrich Peter in 1783; it is given in its entirety in *Records*, 4:1875–85. A modern study of the Revolutionary War period in Salem, published under the auspices of Old Salem, Incorporated, is Hunter James's *The Quiet People of the Land: A Story of the North Carolina Moravians in Revolutionary Times* (Chapel Hill, N.C.: University of North Carolina Press, 1976).

101. Wachovia Memorabilia for 1781, *Records*, 4:1659.

102. Congregation Council Minutes, 26 July 1781, *Records*, 4:1726.

103. A frequent and welcome visitor in Salem, Alexander Martin served as Speaker of the North Carolina Senate and, during the imprisonment of Governor Thomas Burke, as acting governor. During the Assembly meeting in Salem, Burke escaped from prison and appeared at the session. Martin was elected governor of North Carolina in April 1782.

104. *Records*, 4:1727.

105. Congregation Council Minutes, 30 Oct. 1781, *Records*, 4:1734.

106. *Aeltesten Conferenz* Minutes, 31 Oct. 1781, Edmund Schwarze, trans.

107. Ibid.

108. *Aeltesten Conferenz* Minutes, 12 Nov. 1781, *Records*, 4:1736.

109. Ibid.

110. Salem Diary, 13 Nov. 1781, *Records*, 4:1703.

111. Salem Diary, 18 Nov. 1781, *Records*, 4:1704.

112. Salem Diary, 26 Nov. 1781, *Records*, 4:1705.

113. Salem Diary, 27 Nov. 1781, ibid.

114. *Aufseher Collegium* Minutes, Tuesday, 15 Jan. 1782, Erika Huber, trans.

115. Letter dated 7 March 1782 from F. W. Marshall to Count Henry Lewis Von Reuss XXVIII, *Records*, 4:1914.

CHAPTER 3

1. Salem Diary, 19 April 1783. This date is also the eighth anniversary of the Battle of Lexington and Concord (19 April 1775) which marked the beginning of the Revolutionary War, a coincidence noted by Peter in the Wachovia Memorabilia for 1783 (*Records*, 4:1835).

2. *Records*, 4:1834.

3. Manuscript copy filed in the Moravian Archives, Winston-Salem N.C.

4. Salem Diary, 30 June 1783.

5. *Aeltesten Conferenz* Minutes, Monday, 30 June 1783, Item 1: "Da die Obrigkeit das Friedens-Dankfest auf den 4. Jul. proclamirt hat; so wird allen Gemeinen bekommt gemacht werden, dass dieser Tag feyerlich begangen werde, u. jedermann sich an demselben der Arbeit enthalte. Des wegen auch Br. Marschall ein Circulare an die Landgemeinen ausgefertiget hat.
   "Es wird dazu eine öffentliche Predigt seyn das Te Deum gesungen u. ein LMhl. für Erwachsene und Kinder bestellt werden, dazu alle fremde besuchende hinzugelassen werden.
   "Solte der Gouverneur das Fest hier feyern wollen, so wird für ihn eine solenne Tafel im Gasthofe zugerichtet werden."

6. *Aeltesten Conferenz* Minutes, *Mittwoch*, 2 July 1783, Item 2: "*Die Celebration des Friedens-Dankfestes betreffend*; so wird zu Anfang der Predigt um 10 Uhr das Te Deum unter Posaunen-schall gesungen werden. Zum Text der Predigt wurde der 46te Psalm, aus welchem die Losung am 20ten Jan., da die Friedens Praeliminarien unterzeichnet worden, genommen war angesezt. Beym LMhl. um 2 Uhr wird ein musikalischer Dankpsalm gesungen werden, und Abends, nachdem der musikalische Lobgesang: Gelobt seyst Du, der du sizest über Cherubim, auf dem Gemeinsaal gesungen worden, eine Procession mit Musik und Gesang durch den Ort, welcher illuminiret wird, angestellt, und bey der Ruckkunft vor dem Gemeinhaus der Segen des HErrn auf die Gemeine geleget werden."

7. *Records*, 4:1841. The description of the Peace Festival, as recorded in the Salem Diary, is given in its entirety in the original German with English translation as part of the music restoration beginning on p. 42 of this volume.

8. Evidently, one of the major causes of dissension was the scarcity and high cost of butter (*Records*, 4:1835, 1850, 1852).

9. *Aufseher Collegium* Minutes, 10 June 1783, *Records*, 4:1852.

10. *Aeltesten Conferenz* Minutes, 14 June 1783.

11. Ibid., 18 June 1783.

12. Congregation Council Minutes, 19 June 1783, *Records*, 4:1852–53.

13. *Aeltesten Conferenz* Minutes, 25 June 1783.

14. Ibid., 18 June 1783.

15. Ibid., 2 July 1783.

16. Ibid., 9 July 1783.

17. Salem Diary, 4 July 1783.

18. Ibid.

19. Wachovia Memorabilia for 1783, *Records*, 4:1834–35.

20. A pioneer scholar of Moravian Church history, Miss Fries initiated the publication of translated extracts from the archival documents resulting in the series entitled *Records of the Moravians in North Carolina*. By the time of her death, she had prepared seven volumes of translations; her successors, Douglas L. Rights, Minnie J. Smith, and the Right Reverend Kenneth G. Hamilton have added four more volumes to the series.

21. Adelaide L. Fries, "An Early Fourth of July Celebration," *North Carolina Booklet* 15, no. 2 (October 1915): 122–27. Miss Fries claims for Salem the distinction of holding the "first celebration of the Fourth of July by legislative enactment" (p. 123). Numerous unofficial celebrations of the Fourth had taken place in various parts of the country since the signing of the Declaration of Independence. Charles Warren, "Fourth of July Myths," *William and Mary Quarterly*, 3d ser. 2 (July 1945): 237–72, states that "the first official recognition of the day was under the resolve of the Massachusetts legislature in 1781" (p. 258). Warren provides no information concerning the implementation of the resolve; he makes no mention of the 1783 celebration in Salem. In North Carolina, the first celebration under "federal authorization" allegedly was held in New Bern on 4 July 1778 to the accompaniment of the firing of cannon and the drinking of many toasts (Fletcher M. Green, "Listen to the Eagle Scream: One Hundred Years of the Fourth of July in North Carolina [1776–1876], Part I," *North Carolina Historical Review* 31, no. 3 [July 1954], 295–320). The maze of legends surrounding the Fourth of July and its early observances, and the lack of distinguishing definitions of such terms as "official," "legal," "federally authorized," "legislatively enacted," etc., discourages a quick answer to the question of where and when the holiday was first observed. It should be noted, however, that none of the early observances outside Salem has been documented with such careful detail by eyewitnesses, and, as an event of significance in the history of American music, the Salem festival is without peer.

22. Fries, "An Early Fourth of July Celebration," pp. 126–27. Of the six sections translated in the article, only two cite the correct performing group that was assigned to each section of the *Freudenpsalm* (see pp. 24–26 of this volume).

23. The current project began at the behest of Frank Horton, then director of research at Old Salem, Inc., who suggested that a search be made for the music used in the Fourth of July observance. As a part of the bicentennial celebration of the founding of Salem, the music that had been located by that time was performed at Home Moravian Church on Salem Square on 4 July 1966.

24. The festivities surrounding the dedication are described on p. 9 of this volume.

25. The *Gemeinhaus* was razed in the nineteenth century to make room for Salem College's Main Hall which still stands. Much of the information concerning the *Gemeinhaus* and its *Saal* given here is based on the intensive research carried on by Frank L. Horton over a period of seven years, culminating in an unpublished report (1955) in which the exterior and interior design of the *Gemeinhaus* is reconstructed in detail according to information gleaned from the Moravian records. Horton's findings were authenticated almost a decade later when the original drawings of the Salem *Gemeinhaus* were found in the Unity Archives in Herrnhut, Germany. Horton's

report is filed in the offices of Old Salem, Inc., Winston-Salem, N.C.

26. The room dimensions given here are found in the drawings of the *Gemeinhaus* filed in the Unity Archives in Herrnhut, Germany.

27. Members of the congregation who were assigned leadership duties. Lovefeast Dieners prepare and serve the refreshments during the service.

28. Salem Diary, 16 April 1797.

29. *Inventarium von Hausrath Mobilien und Naturalien Bestand des Diacony in Salem 1776 d.11. December.*, Item I, Moravian Archives, Winston-Salem, N.C.

30. Congregation Council Minutes, 9 Dec. 1784: "An old wish was repeated that to encourage better use of the front benches in the congregation *Saal* they should be provided *with backs*" [italics added] (*Records*, 4:2043).

31. *Inventarium . . . 1776.* Twelve benches are listed in 1776; the 1782 revision of the inventory (corrections are made on the 1776 inventory) lists "around 16 benches."

32. *Helfer Conferenz* Minutes, 11 May 1772.

33. *Inventarium . . . 1776*, Item I.

34. Ibid., with the added notation: "nun gestreifte 1781"; Salem Diary, 31 May 1781; "During the past few days new curtains have been hung in the *Saal*" (*Records*, 4:1694).

35. Congregation Council Minutes, 9 June 1780, Erika Huber, trans.: "We renewed the old regulation according to which the rear benches at the organ are to be kept vacant for visitors if the musicians do not play. The young Brethren are to take their seats in the front benches. Married people should sit at the corners."

36. Within a few years, the musicians voiced the need for a raised platform: "Concerning a kind of raised platform for the musicians and singers in the *Gemeinsaal*, there was much discussion and we wish that something of the kind could be made" (*Aufseher Collegium* Minutes, 29 Nov. 1791, Edmund Schwarze, trans.). Later: "The musicians have desired that when the new organ has been installed, we should have something (a platform) raised higher for them and the singers" (*Aufseher Collegium* Minutes, 31 March 1795, Erika Huber, trans.). Almost seven years after their initial request, the musicians were promised that "as soon as the new organ is set up, we will also build some kind of podium" (*Aufseher Collegium* Minutes, 3 April 1798, Erika Huber, trans.).

37. Manuscript filed in the Moravian Archives, Winston-Salem, N.C.

38. The account book labeled "*Gemein Casse Buch 1788*" contains financial records for the years 1783–88 (Moravian Archives, Winston-Salem, N.C.).

39. *Helfer Conferenz* Minutes, 13 May 1776, *Records*, 3:1085. From recipes preserved in the Moravian Archives, Mary Creech, archivist, and Frances Griffin, director of information at Old Salem, Inc., have determined that the "wine made from grapes with *Marticelum*" [also spelled *Marticulum*] is a kind of mead, a fermented mixture of fruit, honey, and water.

40. While it was often used at Lovefeasts, the Elders cautioned that "as much as possible, we want to guard against the use of *Buschwein* at Holy Communion. It is to be used only in the greatest emergency" (*Aeltesten Conferenz* Minutes, 16 May 1780, Edmund Schwarze, trans.). Reasons are not given.

41. *Aeltesten Conferenz* Minutes, 28 May 1781, Edmund Schwarze, trans.

42. *Aufseher Collegium* Minutes, 22 May 1781, *Records*, 4:1721.

43. During the period of dissension in the early part of 1783, one of the complaints voiced by the citizens concerned the price of Lovefeasts: "Brothers and Sisters are not satisfied that for the last Lovefeast with coffee, 8 pens were collected per person, because they think that 6 pens are enough. . . . After calculation, it was found that this could have been done, if necessary" (*Aufseher Collegium* Minutes, 28 Jan. 1783, Erika Huber, trans.).

44. The statistical summary of the Salem Congregation, filed with the Wachovia Memorabilia for 1783, shows that, at the end of the year, there were 186 persons distributed among the following categories:

Salem Congregation consists of:	
23 married couples or	46 persons
2 widowers, 3 widows	5
Single brothers and boys	55
Single sisters and girls	29
Little boys	21
Little girls	14
	170
3 couples living outside	6
Children living outside	10
Total	186

Figures given in Memorabilia for previous years indicate that the population of Salem remained fairly stable, increasing at the rate of approximately ten individuals per year. Thus the population of Salem at the time of the Fourth of July observance probably stood at approximately 180 residents (Moravian Archives, Winston-Salem, N.C.).

45. *Aeltesten Conferenz* Minutes, 30 June 1783, translated on p. 18 of this volume.

46. The account of the Herrnhut peace festival is given in *No. IV. Beylage zur XIIten Woche 1763. Beschreibung der Feyer des Friedens-Danck-Festes der Gemeine in Herrnhuth den 21ten Mart. 1763.* Festivals held in German Moravian communities other than Herrnhut—Barby, Gnadenberg, Gnadenfrey, and Niesky—are described in *No. VI. Beylage zur XIten Woche 1763. Fünfte Sammlung von Gemein-Nachrichten enthaltend I. Die Diaria aus unsern teutschen Gemeinen Mens Mart. 1763.* Manuscript copies of both accounts are preserved in the Moravian Archives in Bethlehem, Pa., and Winston-Salem, N.C. The account of the 1763 Herrnhut peace festival was read at the 1783 Fourth of July service held in Friedland, a Moravian settlement near Salem (*Records*, 4:1873).

47. *No. VI. Beylage zur XIten Woche 1763. 3. Gnadenberg.*

48. The Te Deum was sung at all the 1763 peace festivals, but trombone accompaniment is mentioned only in the accounts of observances in Gnadenberg and Herrnhut.

49. *No. VI. Beylage zur XIten Woche 1763. 7. Barby.*

50. The same composition was performed in Herrnhut to open the day's festivities.

51. *Aeltesten Conferenz* Minutes, 2 July 1783, translated on p. 18 of this volume.

52. The trombones had been used in Salem to accompany the Te Deum on New Year's Day, 1783 (Salem Diary, 1 Jan. 1783, *Records*, 4:1836).

53. At least three manuscript copies of the Lovefeast Psalm text are in existence. One copy, filed with the Salem Diary for 1783, is preserved in the Moravian Archives, Winston-Salem, N.C.; this copy was used as the basic source of the Psalm text in this study. The other copies are filed in the Moravian Music Foundation, Winston-Salem, N.C. (Plate 3) and in the Moravian Archives, Bethlehem, Pa.

54. *No. IV. Beylage zur XIIten Woche 1763 . . . Herrnhut.*

55. *No. VI. Beylage zur XIten Woche 1763. 2. Gnadenfrey.*

56. Though cantatas were also performed in Niesky and Barby, the texts are not included in the descriptions of the 1763 festivals.

57. See p. 5 of this volume and Gombosi, *Catalog of the Johannes Herbst Collection*, pp. viii–x.

58. *Aeltesten Conferenz* Minutes, 2 July 1783, translated on p. 18 of this volume.

59. *Records*, 4:1662–63.

60. The format followed here is based on the manuscript copy filed with the Salem Diary (SA); spelling, capitalization, and punctuation have been retained. Significant differences between the Salem Diary copy and those filed in the Bethlehem Archives (BA) and the Moravian Music Foundation (MMF) are noted, but slight variations in spelling, capitalization, and punctuation have not been indicated. Roman numerals in brackets have been added to facilitate reference to the Psalm text in the discussion of the musical restoration and the musical edition. Two copies of the *Freudenpsalm* text (SA and MMF) appear to be in Friedrich Peter's handwriting; the third copy (BA) was made by an unknown copyist.

61. MMF copy: *Freudenpsalm der Gemeine in Salem/zum Friedens-Dankfest/d. 4. Juli 1783.* (Diagonal strokes mark ends of lines.) BA copy: *Psalm zum Friedensfest der Gemeine/in Salem d. 4. Juli 1783.*

62. MMF copy treats each pair of lines as a single line of text and indicates word or phrase repetitions with ":/:", e.g., "Es ist Friede! :/: freu dich, Volk des HErrn!"

63. *Gem.*=*Gemeine* (congregation).

64. *Alle Brr.*=*Alle Brüder* (all adult male members of the congregation). MMF copy reads: *Brr.*

65. *Alle Schwn.*=*Alle Schwestern* (all adult female members of the congregation). MMF copy reads: *Schwn.*

66. *Alle* (everyone present, including children and guests).

67. This text is identical to that found in the Gnadenfrey account. It does not agree with the text of the musical setting used in Salem. See the score (pp. 70–90) and editorial notes (pp. 192–96) in this volume.

68. MMF copy contains a notation added by another hand: "Mel. Wachet auf." See Plate 3.

69. MMF copy treats "Es ward fast nichts gehört,/Als Feind und Feur und Schwerdt," as one line.

70. The last sentence is omitted in the MMF copy.

71. MMF copy treats "Er allein soll es seyn, unser Gott und HErre;/Ihm gebührt die Ehre!" as one line.

72. MMF copy reads: "Trübsal regte. . . . "

73. This word is underlined in all copies.

74. MMF and BA copies treat each pair of Lines (1+2, 3+4, 5+6, 7+8) as a single line of text.

75. *Beyde Chöre* (both choruses)=Chorus I and II.

76. MMF and BA copies treat "Er hat von Stuhl und Stab/Besiz und lässt nicht ab" as one line.

77. MMF and BA copies treat "Er schenkt voll ein,/Und Gross und Klein" as one line.

78. MMF and BA copies treat each pair of lines (1+2, 3+4, 5+6, 7+8) as a single line of text; line 9 stands alone.

79. MMF copy treats each pair of lines (1+2, 3+4, 5+6, 7+8) as a single line of text.

80. MMF and BA copies read: "lebt."

81. MMF copy reads: *Brr.*

82. MMF copy reads: *Schwn.*

83. One such matter that affected the musical situation in Salem was the placement of an order to Herrnhut for musical supplies: "two D♯ Horns, a good Bass, a set of trombones, and a supply of strings of various kinds" (Congregation Council Minutes, 6 Nov. 1783, *Records*, 4:1857). The instruments arrived two years later (*Aeltesten Conferenz* Minutes, 30 Nov. 1785).

84. Minutes for these meetings are translated on p. 18 of this volume.

85. The complete entry for the 1783 Fourth of July in the Salem Diary is given, along with an English translation, on pp. 42–186 passim of this volume.

86. The specific sources are enumerated and described in the commentary accompanying the edition of the Fourth of July music. See pp. 187–88 of this volume.

87. The choralebook used by the organists at the time of the Fourth of July celebration has not been found.

88. Though it was not a part of the Salem music library in 1783, the Johannes Herbst Collection of annotated musical scores is an invaluable reference tool in a project of this kind, providing information concerning sources and dates of compositions and names of composers. Among the scores in the collection is Gregor's original setting of the liturgy *Gelobt seyst Du* and a copy of the musical setting of the *Danck-Psalm* performed in Herrnhut at the 1763 peace festival.

89. Frances Cumnock, presently engaged in cataloging the Salem Collection, has since identified and thoroughly studied the document.

90. See pp. 191–92 of this volume.

91. C. L. Brau is listed as composer in the 1808 Salem catalogs. See chap. 5, n. 49 of this volume.

92. Modern Moravian hymnals contain a class of tunes for this meter, numbered 597.

93. The term *Arietta* appears on some manuscripts to describe chorale elaborations (Gombosi, *Catalog of the Johannes Herbst Collection*, p. 3, MS 5).

94. Both Moravian versions are adaptations of the opening chorus in Karl Heinrich Graun's *Te Deum Laudamus*, written in celebration of Frederick the Great's victory in the Battle of Prague (1756) and performed at Charlottenburg at the close of the Seven Years' War.

CHAPTER 4

1. Adelaide L. Fries, "An Early Fourth of July Celebration," pp. 126–27.

2. See pp. 9–10, 15 of this volume.

3. See p. 15 of this volume.

4. Salem Collection, Folio 90. The flute parts are not included in the edition since they are post-1783 origin.

CHAPTER 5

1. Filed at the Moravian Music Foundation, Winston-Salem, N.C.

2. This collection is often called the "Single Sisters' Collection" although there is no evidence to support the notion that the library was only for the use of the unmarried women in the congregation.

3. The catalogs described here are in manuscript form, filed at the Moravian Music Foundation, Winston-Salem, N.C. They are the

result of the reorganization of the Salem Collections undertaken by Johannes Reuz in 1808.

4. Before his departure from Salem in 1790, J. F. Peter was asked to prepare a catalog of music, but, if he did so, the catalog has not been recovered (*Aeltesten Conferenz* Minutes, 30 June, 1790, *Records*, 5:2307).

5. Johannes Zahn, *Die Melodien der deutschen evangelischen Kirchenlieder aus den Quellen geschöpft und mitgeteilt* (Gütersloh: Bertelsmann, 1889–93), no. 8562.

6. See p. 4 of this study.

7. *Luther's Works*, ed. Helmut T. Lehmann. Vol. 53, *Liturgy and Hymns*, ed. Ulrich S. Leupold (Philadelphia: Fortress Press, 1964), p. 172. Leupold indicates antiphonal performance by two choirs.

8. The complete text of the *Danck- und Freudenpsalm* is given in *No. IV. Beylage zur XIIten Woche 1763 . . . Herrnhuth*. Musical settings of all the anthems in the *Psalm* are preserved in H 22: "Zum Friedenfest in Hhuth. d. 21. Mart. 1763" (Johannes Herbst Collection, Moravian Music Foundation, Winston-Salem, N.C.).

9. H 13.10: "Zur Christnacht 1760" is an abbreviated version of this anthem; set for SSAB and figured bass, the fourteen-measure instrumental introduction is omitted (Herbst Collection).

10. H 22.3. The score contains only the vocal and string parts. Separate pages with parts for flutes and trumpets are filed with the score (Herbst Collection).

11. *Catalogus . . . nach Ordnung der Nummern . . . 1808* lists the instrumentation as "Tutti, 2 Flauti, 2 Trompi." The wind parts are lacking.

12. Folio 175 contains twelve compositions appropriate for Christmas, which resembles the description of old No. 33 given in the *Anmerckungen . . . 1808*: "Ist eine ganze Christnachts Music, aber sehr unvollständig weil ebenfalls viel zu viel in ein Convolut gedrängt ist" ("Is entirely Christmas music, but very defective because likewise much too much is bunched together in one Convolut"). The principal criticism of the state of the collection voiced in the *Anmerckungen* is the overcrowding of folios and the use of the Organo part as an outside cover for the folio; see the first of three general observations placed at the end of the *Anmerckungen*.

The extant vocal parts and one set of string parts, all of which are labeled "Lebhaft" and are lacking the Christmas chorale, could be the remains of old No. 25 whose description in the *Anmerckungen* contains no reference to Christmas music.

13. This number was added to *Catalogus . . . in alphabetischer Ordnung . . . 1808* after its preparation. The composition was not listed in *Catalogus . . . nach Ordnung der Nummern . . . 1808* until the 1950s when, during an inventory of the collection, a notation was added in pencil.

14. *Anmerckungen . . . 1808*: "Ist unbrauchbar, das einige Stück: *Ehre sey Gott in der Höhe*, von Gregor ausgenommen, welches aber in No. 33 befindlich" ("Is useless, the single piece: *Glory to God in the Highest* by Gregor excepted, but which exists in No. 33"). Several additional parts and fragments of parts, some of nineteenth- or twentieth-century provenance, are scattered throughout the Salem Congregation music; during the present cataloging project under the direction of Frances Cumnock, these pages have been assigned numbers including: S 18.7, S 26.7, S 508.2, SS 21.7, and SS 92.6.

15. Gombosi, *Catalog of the Johannes Herbst Collection*, p. xi.

16. This manuscript is not listed in *Catalogus . . . für das Schwestern-Sänger Chor . . . nach Ordnung der Nummern . . . 1808*.

17. See remarks under 2. S 168 (p. 190).

18. Zahn, *Die Melodien der deutschen evangelischen Kirchenlieder*, no. 7341a.

19. H 14: "Zum·4. May, 1761" (Herbst Collection).

20. *No. VI. Beylage zur XIten Woche 1763. 2. Gnadenfrey.*

21. *Anmerckungen . . . 1808* attributes this composition to Geisler. *Catalogus . . . nach Ordnung der Nummern . . . 1808* lists Graun as the composer. In *Catalogus . . . in alphabetischer Ordnung . . . 1808,* Geisler's name has been crossed out and "aus Grauns Te Deum" inserted.

22. *Catalogus . . . für das Schwestern-Sänger Chor . . . in alphabetischer Ordnung . . . 1808* lists Geisler as the composer. *Catalogus für das Schwestern-Sänger Chor . . . nach Ordnung der Nummern . . . 1808* contains this citation: "Geisler aus Grauns Tod Jesu [!]."

23. This manuscript contains musical settings for all the anthems contained in the *Danck-Psalm* performed in Gnadenfrey on 13 March 1763; unspecified portions of the *Danck-Psalm* were performed the following Sunday (20 March 1763) in Gnadenberg as part of the peace festival held in that community. See *No. VI. Beylage zur XIten Woche 1763. 2. Gnadenfrey [and] 3. Gnadenberg.*

24. On the other hand, copyists preparing the *Freudenpsalm* text for distribution to the congregation for their use during the Lovefeast and for inclusion in the diary probably worked from the written text contained in the account of the 1763 peace festival held in Gnadenfrey (*No. VI. Beylage zur XIten Woche 1763. 2. Gnadenfrey*). As a part of the church archives, this account was in the custody of J. F. Peter and stored in his living quarters (*Aeltesten Conferenz Minutes,* 4 Dec. 1782).

25. Zahn, *Die Melodien der deutschen evangelischen Kirchenlieder*, no. 8405a.

26. *No. VI. Beylage zur XIten Woche 1763. 2. Gnadenfrey.*

27. See note 23 above.

28. Zahn, *Die Melodien der deutschen evangelischen Kirchenlieder*, no. 4791.

29. *No. VI. Beylage zur XIten Woche 1763. 2. Gnadenfrey.*

30. See note 23 above.

31. Zahn, *Die Melodien der deutschen evangelischen Kirchenlieder*, no. 7886b.

32. *No. VI. Beylage zur XIten Woche 1763. 2. Gnadenfrey.*

33. See note 23 above.

34. Karl Straube, *Choralvorspiele alter Meister* (Leipzig: Peters, 1907), pp. 80–83.

35. Two versions of this composition by Gregor are preserved in the Herbst Collection. H 21.2: "Zum 2. Febr. 1763" contains a setting of the text, "Siehe, du hast Lust zur Wahrheit" (GG 901, stanza 7), for SSAB, flute, bassoon, and strings; H 26.1: "Zum Gr. Agnes Geburts-tag am 14. May 1763" is a setting for SS and strings of the text, "Ach Schönster unter allen" (GG 647, stanza 2). The latter version is the basis for the settings preserved in the Salem Collections.

36. *Catalogus . . . nach Ordnung der Nummern . . . 1808* lists this composition as a "Duetto."

37. The description of this composition in *Anmerckungen . . . 1808* reads: "Schön und gut, nur muss man annehmen, dass das Stück (*Ach Schönster unter allen*) ächten Musicis gar sehr, sonst niemanden gefällt" ["Beautiful and good, only one must admit that the piece (*Ach Schönster unter allen*) pleases trained musicians very much, but no one else"].

38. See note 35 above.

39. Ibid.

40. *Catalogus . . . für das Schwestern-Sänger Chor . . . in alphabetischer Ordnung . . . 1808* lists this composition, but it does not appear in *Catalogus . . . für das Schwestern-Sänger Chor . . . nach Ordnung der Nummern . . . 1808* or among the list of compositions given on the folder containing ss 80.

41. Zahn, *Die Melodien der deutschen evangelischen Kirchenlieder*, no. 8405a.

42. Ibid., no. 1062a.

43. Ibid., no. 5741b.

44. *No. IV. Beylage zur XIIten Woche 1763 . . . Herrnhuth.*

45. Zahn, *Die Melodien der deutschen evangelischen Kirchenlieder*, no. 6923.

46. The complete text of the *Danck- und Freudenpsalm* is given in *No. IV. Beylage zur XIIten Woche 1763 . . . Herrnhuth.* Musical settings of all the anthems in the Psalm are preserved in H 22: "Zum Friedensfest in Hhuth. d. 21. Mart. 1763" (Herbst Collection).

47. It is clear from the description of old No. 69 given in the *Anmerckungen* that the contents of that manuscript were rearranged and even altered in the ensuing cataloging project. The *Anmerckungen* lists but two composers as being represented in old No. 69 (Gregor and J. F. Peter); *Catalogus . . . nach Ordnung der Nummern . . . 1808,* prepared after the reorganization of the collection, gives three names (Jeremiah Dencke, Gregor, and Peter). In the vocal parts, this composition appears as the third composition, following anthems numbered 1 and 2; however, the instrumental parts contain the compositions in the order they are given in the *Catalogus,* i.e., "Dass in unserm Lande" is numbered 10, following anthems 8 and 9. The inference that the vocal parts are a part of the old Salem Collection because of their numerical arrangement is fortified by the fact that these parts are in full agreement with the score of the Herrnhut peace festival music. The instrumental parts, on the other hand, in addition to their new numerical order, are transposed a step higher than the original key, suggesting that they are of later origin; the entry for old No. 69 in *Anmerckungen . . . 1808* also mentions the fact that a new organ part had been recently copied, establishing the post-1783 origin of that part.

48. See note 46 above.

49. This setting is attributed to C. L. Brau in all extant Salem sources, i.e., the *Anmerckungen . . . 1808,* the four catalogs prepared in 1808, and the folios containing the manuscripts. It should be noted, however, that all these sources were prepared some twenty-five years after the 1783 Fourth of July observance, and, further, they are the work of one man, Johannes Reuz. In the earlier catalogs of the Lititz Collection (1795) and the Bethlehem Collection (1804), Johann Christian Geisler is cited as the composer. According to Johannes Herbst who was living in Europe at the time of its composition, Geisler prepared this anthem for the dedication of the new *Saal* in Zeist, Holland, on 20 October 1768 (Gombosi, *Catalog of the Johannes Herbst Collection,* p. 85, MS 117.3). The weight of evidence seems to favor Geisler as the composer of this anthem.

50. Zahn, *Die Melodien der deutschen evangelischen Kirchenlieder*, no. 8405a.

51. *No. IV. Beylage zur XIIten Woche 1763 . . . Herrnhuth.*

52. The quoted portion of Martin Luther's hymn "Aus tiefer Noth schrey ich zu dir" is the last half of the fourth stanza.

53. This tune is one of the melodies discarded by Gregor in his *Choralbuch* (1784). See p. 187. I am indebted to Margaret Leinbach Kolb, who procured the microfilm copy of the Grimm *Choralbuch* manuscript for the Moravian Music Foundation, for her assistance in locating and identifying the source of this tune.

CRSOURCES and DOCUMENTS

MANUSCRIPTS, BOOKS, ARTICLES

Aeltesten Conferenz. Protocoll [Elders Conference. Minutes]. 1769–90. MSS, Moravian Archives, Winston-Salem, N.C.

————. Extracts translated by Edmund Schwarze. Typewritten. N.d. Moravian Archives, Winston-Salem, N.C.

Anmerckungen beym durchsehen der Musicalien der Gemeine in Salem. Mart. 1808. MS, Moravian Music Foundation, Winston-Salem, N.C.

Aufseher Collegium. Protocoll [Board of Overseers. Minutes]. 1772–90. MSS, Moravian Archives, Winston-Salem, N.C.

————. Extracts translated by Erika Huber. Typewritten. N.d. Moravian Archives, Winston-Salem, N.C.

————. Extracts translated by Edmund Schwarze. Typewritten. N.d. Moravian Archives, Winston-Salem, N.C.

Bagge, Traugott, trans. A Short Historical Account about the Present Constitution of the Protestant Unity of Brethren of the Augustan Confession. Translated from the German Edition, Printed at Francfort and Leipzig [in] 1774. 1778. MS, Moravian Archives, Winston-Salem, N.C.

Cassa-Buch der Musikalischen Collecte seit 1780 [Music Accounts]. 1780–87. MSS, Moravian Music Foundation, Winston-Salem, N.C.

Catalogus der Gemein Musicken für das Schwestern-Sänger Chor der Gemeine in Salem in alphabetischer Ordnung verfertiget im Jahr 1808. MS, Moravian Music Foundation, Winston-Salem, N.C.

Catalogus der Gemein Musicken für das Schwestern-Sänger Chor der Gemeine in Salem nach Ordnung der Nummern verfertiget im Jahr 1808. MS, Moravian Music Foundation, Winston-Salem, N.C.

Catalogus der Gemein Musicken welche der Gemeine in Salem gehören, in alphabetischer Ordnung: verfertiget im Jahr 1808. MS, Moravian Music Foundation, Winston-Salem, N.C.

Catalogus der Gemein Musicken welche der Gemeine in Salem gehören, nach Ordnung der Nummern verfertiget im Jahr 1808. MS, Moravian Music Foundation, Winston-Salem, N.C.

Catalogus der Gemein-Musik der Gemeine in Litiz gehörig verfertiget den 5ten. Januar 1795. MS, Moravian Archives, Bethlehem, Pa.

Des Diarii des Gemein Hauses 63. 12te Woche in Hhuth [Extract from the Herrnhut Diary, March 1763]. MS, Moravian Archives, Winston-Salem, N.C.

Diarium der Colone, welche am 29. April 1762 von Bethlehem über Philadelphia und Wilmingtown, nach Bethabara auf der Wachau, abreistren [Travel Diary, now bound in volume labeled Wachovia Diary and Memorabilia 1762]. MS, Moravian Archives, Winston-Salem, N.C.

Diarium der ersten Colonne Led. Brüder nach Nord Carolina. 1753–55. MS, Moravian Archives, Winston-Salem, N.C.

Diarium der Gemeine in der Wachau. 1762–70. MSS, Moravian Archives, Winston-Salem, N.C.

Diarium der Gemeine in Salem. 1771–97. MSS, Moravian Archives, Winston-Salem, N.C.

Diarium der kleines Pilger Gemeine die 2ten. Octobr. 1755. ihr Reise von Bethlehem nach Wachau in North Carolina antrat [Travel Diary, now bound in volume labeled Wachovia Diary 1755]. MS, Moravian Archives, Winston-Salem, N.C.

Diarium der Led. Brr. in Wachau, 1755. MS, Moravian Archives, Winston-Salem, N.C.

Diarium von Bethabara u. Bethanien, 1762. MS, Moravian Archives, Winston-Salem, N.C.

Diarium von dem Gemeinlein in Bethabara, 1773. MS, Moravian Archives, Winston-Salem, N.C.

Die Armen Casse in Salem [Charity Accounts], 1777–78. MS, Moravian Archives, Winston-Salem, N.C.

Die Bürgerliche Casse in Salem [Municipal Accounts], 1780–83. MSS, Moravian Archives, Winston-Salem, N.C.

Die Gemein-Casse in Salem [Congregation Accounts, filed under "Salem Church Accounts"], 1773–88. MSS, Moravian Archives, Winston-Salem, N.C.

Die Gemein Diaconie in Salem [Diacony Accounts], 1779–80. MS, Moravian Archives, Winston-Salem, N.C.

Die Gemeine in Salem für deren Liebes-Mahl Casse [Lovefeast Accounts], 1782–84. MSS, Moravian Archives, Winston-Salem, N.C.

Extract des Diarii der Gemeinen in der Wachau. 1783. MS, Moravian Archives, Winston-Salem, N.C.

Freudenpsalm der Gemeine in Salem zum Friedens-Dankfest d. 4. Juli 1783. MS, The Moravian Music Foundation, Winston-Salem, N.C.

Freudenpsalm Der Gemeine in Salem zum Friedens-Dankfeste. d. 4. Juli 1783. MS, Moravian Archives, Winston-Salem, N.C.

Fries, Adelaide L. "An Early Fourth of July Celebration." *North Carolina Booklet* 15, no. 2 (October 1915): 122–27.

————; Rights, Douglas L.; Smith, Minnie J.; Hamilton, Kenneth G., eds. *Records of the Moravians in North Carolina.* 11 vols. Raleigh: State Department of Archives and History, 1922–.

Gemeinrath. Protocoll [Congregation Council. Minutes], 1774–90. MSS, Moravian Archives, Winston-Salem, N.C.

_____. Extracts translated by Erika Huber. Typewritten. N.d. Moravian Archives, Winston-Salem, N.C.

Gombosi, Marilyn P., ed. *Catalog of the Johannes Herbst Collection*. Chapel Hill: University of North Carolina Press, 1970.

Green, Fletcher M. "Listen to the Eagle Scream: One Hundred Years of the Fourth of July in North Carolina (1776–1876), Part I." *North Carolina Historical Review* 31, no. 3 (July 1954): 295–320.

Gregor, Christian, ed. *Choral-Buch, enthaltend alle zu dem Gesangbuche der evangelischen Brüder-Gemeinen vom Jahre 1778 gehörige Melodien*. Leipzig, 1784.

_____. *Gesangbuch zum Gebrauch der evangelischen Brüdergemeinen*. Barby, 1778.

Grimm, Johann Daniel, ed.? *Choral-Buch, Darinnen enthalten alle Melodien, so in den Brüder Gesängen vorkommen nebst einern Register über dieselben*. [1755]. MS, Archiv der Brüderunität, Herrnhut, Germany. Microfilm copy, Moravian Music Foundation, Winston-Salem, N.C.

Grosse Helfer Conferenz für Ganz. Protocoll [Helfer Conferenz. Minutes], 1765–90. MSS, Moravian Archives, Winston-Salem, N.C.

_____. Extracts translated by Edmund Schwarze. Typewritten. N.d. Moravian Archives, Winston-Salem, N.C.

Horton, Frank L. "Supplementary Notes regarding the Drawing and Plans Prepared in 1955 of the Congregation House in Salem." Typewritten. Old Salem, Incorporated, Winston-Salem, N.C.

Hoyt, William K. "The Lot, the Youth and the Schobers." In *The Three Forks of Muddy Creek*. Volume 1. Edited by Frances Griffin. Winston-Salem: Old Salem, Incorporated, 1974.

Inventarium der Mobillien u. Instrumente im Gemein Haus Bethabara d. 14. Aug. 1766. MS, Moravian Archives, Winston-Salem, N.C.

Inventarium von Hausrath Mobilien und Naturalien Bestand des Diacony in Salem d. 11. December 1776. With 1781 and 1782 revisions. MS, Moravian Archives, Winston-Salem, N.C.

Luther, Martin. *Luther's Works*. Edited by Helmut T. Lehmann. Vol. 53, *Liturgy and Hymns*, edited by Ulrich S. Leupold. Philadelphia: Fortress Press, 1964.

Marshall [Marschall], Friedrich Wilhelm. Letter to Count Henry Lewis Von Reuss XXVIII, 7 March 1782. MS, Moravian Archives, Winston-Salem, N.C.

_____. Report to Unity Elders Conference, August–November 1772. MS, Moravian Archives, Winston-Salem, N.C.

Martin, Alexander. Proclamation, 18 June 1783. MS, Moravian Archives, Winston-Salem, N.C.

Memorabilien der Gemeinen in der Wachau, 1772–83. MSS, Moravian Archives, Winston-Salem, N.C.

No. IV. Beylage zur XIIten Woche 1763. Beschreibung der Feyer des Friedens-Danck-Festes der Gemeine in Herrnhuth den 21ten Mart. 1763. MS, Moravian Archives, Winston-Salem, N.C., and Moravian Archives, Bethlehem, Pa.

No. VI. Beylage zur XIten Woche 1763. Fünfte Sammlung von Gemein-Nachrichten enthaltend I. Die Diaria aus unsern teutschen Gemeinen Mens. Mart. 1763. MS, Moravian Archives, Winston-Salem, N.C., and Moravian Archives, Bethlehem, Pa.

Peter, Friedrich. *Lebenslauf*. MS, Moravian Archives, Bethlehem, Pa.

Psalm zum Friedensfest der Gemeine in Salem d. 4. Juli 1783. MS, Moravian Archives, Bethlehem, Pa.

Rechnung der Musikalischen Cassa d. 8. Februar 1781. MS, Moravian Music Foundation, Winston-Salem, N.C.

Single Brothers' Miscellaneous Accounts, 1774–90. MSS, Moravian Archives, Winston-Salem, N.C.

Spangenberg, August Gottlieb. *Kurzgefasste historische Nachricht von der gegenwärtigen Verfassung der evangelischen Brüderunität augspurgischer Confession*. Frankfurt, 1774.

Straube, Karl. *Choralvorspiele alter Meister*. Leipzig: Peters, 1907.

Strudwick, Samuel. Letter to Traugott Bagge, 26 August 1777. MS, Moravian Archives, Winston-Salem, N.C.

Verzeichniss der Gemein-Musikalien in Bethlehem verfertiget im Jahr 1804. MS, Moravian Archives, Bethlehem, Pa.

Verzeichniss der Gemein-Musikalien in Nazareth verfertiget im Jahr 1804. MS, Moravian Archives, Bethlehem, Pa.

Warren, Charles. "Fourth of July Myths." *William and Mary Quarterly*. 3d ser. 2 (July 1945): 237–72.

Zahn, Johannes. *Die Melodien der deutschen evangelischen Kirchenlieder aus den Quellen geschöpft und mitgeteilt*. 6 vols. Gütersloh: Bertelsmann, 1889–93.

MUSIC MANUSCRIPT COLLECTIONS

Johannes Herbst Collection. Scores. Moravian Music Foundation, Winston-Salem, N.C.

Lititz Congregation Collection. Parts. Moravian Archives, Bethlehem, Pa.

Salem Choralebooks. Parts. Moravian Music Foundation, Winston-Salem, N.C.

Salem Congregation Collection. Parts. Moravian Music Foundation, Winston-Salem, N.C.

Salem Sisters Collection. Parts. Moravian Music Foundation, Winston-Salem, N.C.

ᏟᏟINDEX